Holt

ELEMENTARY SCIENCE

Joseph Abruscato   Joan Wade Fossaceca

Jack Hassard   Donald Peck

HOLT, RINEHART AND WINSTON, PUBLISHERS
New York • Toronto • London • Sydney

THE AUTHORS

Joseph Abruscato
Associate Dean
College of Education and Social Services
University of Vermont
Burlington, Vermont

Joan Wade Fossaceca
Teacher
Pointview Elementary School
Westerville City Schools
Westerville, Ohio

Jack Hassard
Professor
College of Education
Georgia State University
Atlanta, Georgia

Donald Peck
Supervisor of Science
Woodbridge Township School District
Woodbridge, New Jersey

Photo and art acknowledgments appear on pages 311 and 312.
Cover photograph by California Institute of Technology and
    Carnegie Institution of Washington.

ISBN: 0-03-040561-0
901234   071   987654321

THE CONSULTANTS

Content Consultants

Edward E. C. Clebsch, Ph.D.
Professor of Botany
University of Tennessee
Knoxville, Tennessee

Jerry Faughn, Ph.D.
Professor of Physics
Eastern Kentucky University
Richmond, Kentucky

Ellen M. Herron, Ph.D.
Assistant Director
Lamont-Doherty Geological Observatory
Palisades, New York

Margaret A. LeMone, Ph.D.
Scientist
National Center for Atmospheric Research
Boulder, Colorado

W. T. Lippincott, Ph.D.
Professor of Chemistry
University of Arizona
Tucson, Arizona

Gary Peterson, D.A.
Assoc. Professor of Biology
South Dakota State University
Brookings, South Dakota

Arne E. Slettebak
Professor of Astronomy
Ohio State University
Columbus, Ohio

Gordon Taylor
Principal
Estey School
Saskatoon, Saskatchewan

Teacher Consultants

Peggy Ann Archacki
Assistant Supervisor of Science
Cleveland Public Schools
Cleveland, Ohio

Thomas L. Beck
Teacher
Evening Street Elementary School
Worthington, Ohio

Lynn T. Cluff
Teacher
Central School
South Burlington, Vermont

Linda Coffey, Ph.D.
Director of Early Childhood/Ed.
Broward County Public Schools
Broward County, Florida

Marcia Lambek
Teacher
School One
Scotch Plains, New Jersey

Carole Rutland
Teacher
Muscogee County Public Schools
Columbus, Georgia

Judy Woodward
Science Advisor
Delevan Science Center
Los Angeles City Schools
Los Angeles, California

Rina Zucker
Teacher
Ashford Elementary School
Houston, Texas

Reading Consultants

Paul Greenfield
Associate Professor
English and Humanities
Dutchess Community College
Poughkeepsie, New York

Judith Linscott Martin
Reading Specialist
Montgomery County Public Schools
Montgomery County, Maryland

Evelyn Mason
Elementary Language Arts Supervisor
Indianapolis Public Schools
Indianapolis, Indiana

PILOT SCHOOLS

We gratefully acknowledge the help of the teachers and students who field-tested portions of the Holt Elementary Science program in the spring of 1977. Their comments and criticisms were used to improve the program. The field teachers were:

Margaret Rodriquez
Encinal School
Morgan Hill, CA

Viola Sando
Murphy School
Stamford, CT

Lenore Ambrose
Palmetto El Sch
Miami, FL

Judy Kaplan
Lake Stevens El Sch
OpaLock, FL

Beth Williams
Laura Childs El Sch
Bloomington, IN

David Allen
Howard C. Reiche Sch
Portland, ME

Stephanie Barnhart
Immac Heart of Mary Sch
Towson, MD

John Cooney
Mill Swan El Sch
Worcester, MA

Eileen Martin
Stearns School
Pittsfield, MA

Phil Maines
Fountain El Sch
Grand Rapids, MI

Olivia McKinney
Vernor El Sch
Detroit, MI

Ellen Stob
Hillcrest El Sch
Grand Rapids, MI

Dennis Davis
Portland El Sch
Richfield, MN

Gary Hawkins
Cambridge El Sch
Cambridge, MN

M. Foster
Green Trails Sch
Chesterfield, MO

A. J. Sullivan
Ferguson Florissant Sch Dist
Ferguson, MO

Rick Ashworth
Choteau School
Choteau, MT

Nancy Ritter
Fort Benton Sch
Ft. Benton, MT

J. Ely
Burgess School
Berlin, NH

Edward Douglas
Sumner El Sch
Camden, NJ

Nancy Hearst
Pennypacher El Sch
Willingboro, NJ

Lee Ferrera
St. Jerome Sch
Brooklyn, NY

Robert Kase
Public School 178
Jamaica, NY

Lois Parker
Bloomfield El Sch
Holcomb, NY

Lorraine Sharp
95th Street School
Niagara Falls, NY

Paul Snyder
93rd Street School
Niagara Falls, NY

Helen Suchy
Theo Roosevelt El Sch
Binghamton, NY

Edward Wianecki
School 43
Buffalo, NY

Patricia Brazas
Peck El Sch
Greensboro, NC

Ann Schwabeland
Irving Park El Sch
Greensboro, NC

Bernice Perry
Brooks El Sch
Raleigh, NC

John Foley
Lewis and Clark Sch
Fargo, ND

Manna Hay
Arlington Sch
Toledo, OH

Charles Knepshield
Taft El Sch
Middletown, OH

Dawn Rowe
Brush El Sch
Grafton, OH

Ross Neidich
West Branch El Sch
Bradford, PA

Frank Rice, Jr.
Westview El Sch
Spartanburg, SC

Wilma Todd
Cooper El Sch
Garland, TX

James Goodwin
East Salem Sch
Salem, VA

Dean Rickabaugh
Highland Park Sch
Roanoke, VA

Patricia Kinner
St. Aemilian's Sch
Milwaukee, WI

Kathryn Lee
Falk El Sch
Madison, WI

Many thanks also to the principals, supervisors, and science coordinators who assisted in the arrangements for the field test.

CONTENTS

Most people in this country do not live near an ocean. Do you? Many people have never seen the ocean. Have you? How did it look to you?

The ocean is a frontier. What do you think that sentence means? Seventy percent of the earth is covered by ocean water. Many things are known about the ocean. There are many things scientists can still learn about the ocean. It is a place where exploration is new. In this unit you will find out about the ocean.

OCEAN FRONTIERS

CHAPTER 1

THE OCEAN

1 THE OCEAN BOTTOM

What do you think is on the bottom of the ocean? Long ago pirates hoped they could find buried treasures there. People have always wondered about the ocean bottom. Is it flat? How deep is it? When you finish this lesson, you should be able to:

○ Name and describe five parts of the ocean bottom and floor.

○ Tell the name for people who study the ocean.

A. Your teacher will give you a model ocean.

B. Make a chart like the one shown.

C. Place your ruler straight in the water until it hits the bottom.

1. How many centimeters (inches) is it from the bottom to the surface of the water?

D. On your chart, make an X above trial 1 opposite the number that shows the distance between the bottom and the surface of the water.

E. Repeat steps C and D nine times. For each trial place the ruler at different points across the length of the model.

F. Draw a line connecting the X's on your chart.

Materials
model ocean
paper
pencil
ruler

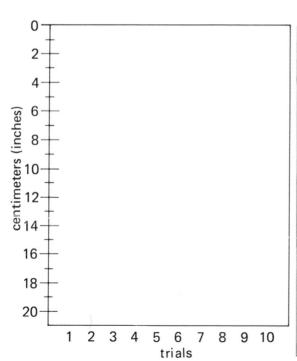

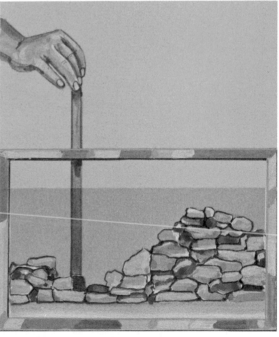

The diagram you made of the model ocean shows that your ocean bottom has high and low places. Scientists have found out the same thing about the real ocean bottom. It also has high and low places.

The ocean bottom is divided into three main parts. The first part is called the **continental shelf** (kahn-tin-**nen**-tal). The *continental shelf* starts where the part of the land we live on ends. It is part of the continent, but it is covered with water. The continental shelf is the shallowest part of the ocean. Its average depth is about 60 meters (200 feet).

At the end of the continental shelf, the land plunges downward sharply. This part of the ocean bottom is called the **continental slope**. The ocean may be 3,050 m (10,000 ft) deep at the bottom of the *continental slope*. Why do you think the word *slope* is used to describe what occurs?

The third part of the ocean bottom, called the **ocean floor,** begins where the continental slope ends. The *ocean floor* covers most of the ocean bottom. Part of the ocean floor is flat. This flat part is called the **abyssal plain.** (ah-**biss**-al).

At one time, scientists thought the whole ocean bottom was smooth and flat. Today we know there is a huge chain of moutains on the ocean bottom. This mountain chain is called the **mid-ocean ridge**. The *mid-ocean ridge* is about 65,000 kilometers (40,000 miles) long and runs through every ocean on the earth.

Look at the map of the ocean bottom. It shows the northern part of the Atlantic Ocean with all the water removed. Can you find the continental shelf, continental slope, *abyssal plain*, and mid-ocean ridge?

Scientists have discovered a giant crack down the center of the mid-ocean ridge. The crack is 13 km to 48 km (8 to 30 mi) wide and is more than 1.6 km (1 mi) deep in some places. Can you find this long crack in the mid-ocean ridge on the map?

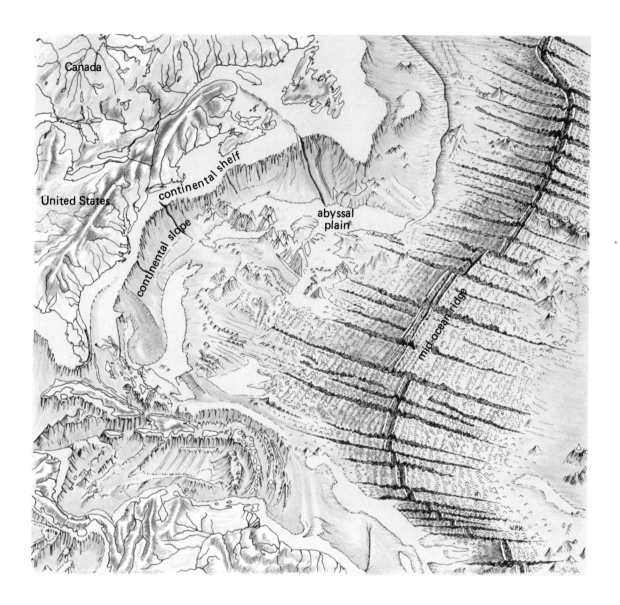

Canada

United States

continental shelf

continental slope

abyssal plain

mid-ocean ridge

V.P.K.

Continental shelf: The part of the continent covered with water.

Continental slope: The sloping part of the ocean bottom.

Ocean floor: The part of the ocean bottom that begins where the continental slope ends.

Abyssal plain: The flat part of the ocean floor.

Mid-ocean ridge: Mountain chain on the ocean floor.

Oceanographers:
Scientists who study
the oceans.

Scientists who study the oceans are called **oceanographers** (oh-shun-**nog**-**graf**-furs). There are many kinds of *oceanographers*. Some study the plains and mountains of the ocean bottom. Some study the plant and animal life in the ocean. Others study the ocean water or discover new ways to explore the ocean.

MAIN IDEAS

The ocean bottom consists of the continental shelf, continental slope, and ocean floor. The ocean floor has two parts: the abyssal plain and the mid-ocean ridge.

QUESTIONS

Write your answers on a sheet of paper.

1. What are the three main parts of the ocean bottom?

2. Name two parts of the ocean floor.

3. Name the part of the ocean bottom described in each phrase below.
   a. part of the continent, but covered with water
   b. the land that plunges sharply
   c. covers most of the ocean bottom
   d. flat part of ocean floor
   e. chain of mountains on ocean floor

6

2 SALT AND SEDIMENTS

Water, water, everywhere, and not a drop to drink! Why can't the woman in the boat drink the ocean water? People can drink only fresh water. Only three percent of the water on the earth is fresh. Ninety-seven percent is salty.

When you finish this lesson, you should be able to:

○ Explain why ocean water is salty.

○ Tell the name given to materials that settle on the ocean bottom.

○ Tell where these materials are found.

Sodium chloride: A salt.

Rivers flow from mountain lakes to the oceans. As the rivers flow over the land, they carry materials from the land. Some of these materials are salts. The salts are dissolved in the water. One kind of salt rivers carry is **sodium chloride** (so-dee-um **klor**-ide). The salt you use on your food is *sodium chloride*. When a river empties into an ocean, the salt mixes with the ocean water.

Ocean water is heated by the sun. As ocean water is heated, it evaporates. The water changes from a liquid to a gas. What happens to the salt in this evaporating water?

A. Dissolve $\frac{1}{4}$ teaspoon of salt in a paper cup half filled with water.

B. Pour about three drops of the salted water on the inside of the jar lid.

C. Place the lid in the sunlight or other warm place for at least 10 minutes.

1. What happened to the water? Why?

2. What is left on the jar lid? How can you test to find out?

Materials
jar lid
paper cup
salt
teaspoon

When the water on your jar lid evaporated, salt was left behind. The same thing has been happening for millions of years as ocean water evaporates. Salt is left behind. The amount of salt in the ocean is not the same all over. Near the equator, ocean water is saltier than at the poles. Why do you think this is true?

If ocean water is always evaporating why don't the oceans dry up? As long as rivers keep flowing and rain falls, the oceans will have a supply of water.

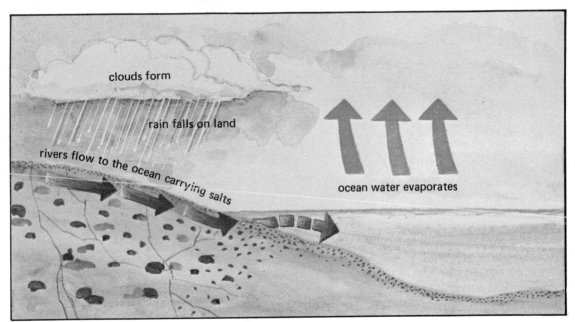

clouds form

rain falls on land

rivers flow to the ocean carrying salts

ocean water evaporates

Sediments: Sand, clay, and other materials that settle in water.

Submarine canyon: A groove cut in the continental shelf and slope.

Salts are not the only materials carried to the oceans by rivers. Rivers also carry sand, mud, clay, and rocks. These materials are called **sediments** (sed-eh-ments). *Sediments* settle to the bottom in still water. Most sediments settle close to the shore and form beaches. Other sediments are carried farther out. They settle on the continental shelf. Sometimes the sediments on the shelf move or slide. They slide down the continental slope. This movement cuts grooves in the shelf and slope. These grooves are called **submarine canyons** (sub-mar-reen **kan**-yons). Look at the diagram. Can you find the *submarine canyon*? Some of this sediment stays at the bottom of the slope. Some of the sediment moves farther out and settles on the abyssal plain.

Another type of sediment on the ocean bottom comes from plants and animals. When animals and plants die, their remains settle on the ocean bottom. They become part of the layers of sediment on the ocean bottom.

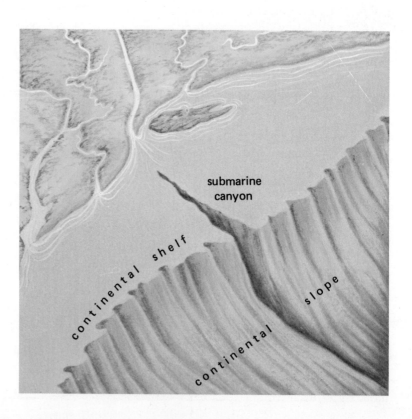

submarine canyon

continental shelf

continental slope

continental

Rivers carry salts and other sediments to the oceans. Some sediments are deposited near the shore on the continental shelf and on the abyssal plains. Sediments that slide over the continental shelf and slope form submarine canyons.

QUESTIONS

Write your answers on a sheet of paper.

1. Why is the ocean salty? Name a salt.
2. What are sediments? How do they get to the ocean?
3. Below is a map of the ocean bottom. Sediments may settle on the parts labeled A, B, and C. Give the real name for these labeled parts. What happens when sediments slide down parts A and B?

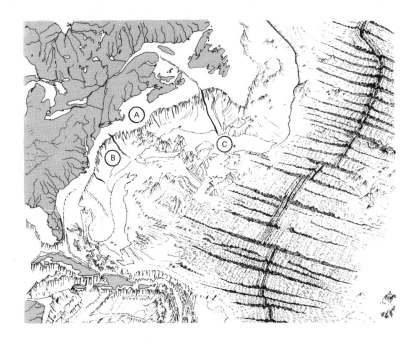

3 CHANGES IN THE OCEAN FLOOR

Long ago, people thought the world was flat. When explorers, such as Christopher Columbus, said the world was round, people did not believe them. Fifty years ago, if oceanographers said the ocean floor was spreading, people would not have believed them either.

When you fnish this lesson, you should be able to:

○ Tell why scientists believe the ocean floor is spreading.

○ Name islands formed by the mid-ocean ridge.

Scientists think it is very hot inside the earth. It is believed to be so hot there that rock within the earth can melt, or become **molten** (mol-ten). This hot, *molten* rock in the earth can move up toward the earth's surface under the giant crack in the mid-ocean ridge. When the molten rock breaks through the surface, it forms new ocean floor on both sides of the crack. The new ocean floor pushes against sections of the old floor. Many scientists think that the old floor on both sides of the crack moves. Therefore, scientists say the ocean floor is spreading away from the crack.

Molten: Melted by heat.

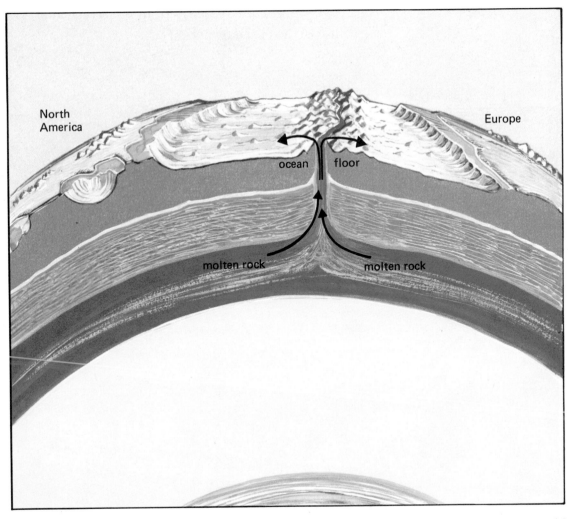

Scientists believe that the Atlantic Ocean is getting wider by 3 cm (about 1 in.) each year. The continents of Europe and North America are moving apart. The idea of sea floor spreading explains these changes.

What do you think is happening to the Pacific Ocean? As the Atlantic Ocean spreads and the land moves apart, the Pacific Ocean is getting narrower. As the Pacific narrows, its ocean floor moves downward under the land that borders the ocean. Deep ocean valleys called **trenches** are formed. *Trenches* are some of the deepest places in the ocean. The drawing below shows how trenches are formed.

Trenches: Deep ocean valleys.

Look at the world map. The red lines show where most ocean trenches are located. In which ocean do you see most of the ocean trenches?

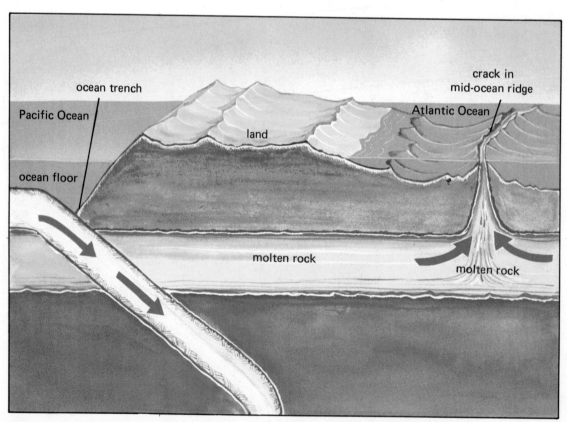

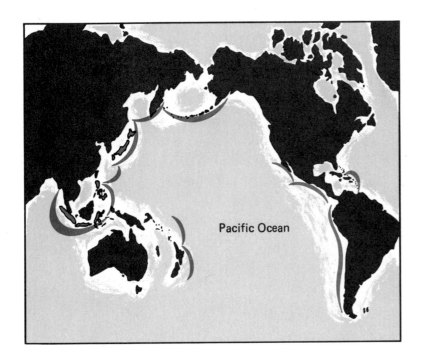

Pacific Ocean

The molten rock that pushes up under the mid-ocean ridge cools and hardens, forming mountains. Sometimes these moutains are so high they stick out of the water. We call them islands. The **Azores** (a-zorz) are a group of islands in the North Atlantic Ocean. The *Azores* are really the tops of mountains that are part of the mid-ocean ridge.

Azores: Islands in the North Atlantic Ocean.

Hot molten rock in the earth can push up through the crack in the mid-ocean ridge. Scientists think that the molten rock forms new ocean floor, which pushes the old floor away from the crack. They think that the ocean floor is spreading.

QUESTIONS

Write your answers on a sheet of paper.

1. Why does rock in the earth become molten?
2. How do scientists think molten rock causes the ocean floor to spread?
3. Name a group of islands formed by the mid-ocean ridge.

SOMETHING EXTRA

The picture at the right is of a famous oceanographer. Do you know his name? With his crew and ship, the *Calypso*, he has studied the oceans all over the world. This famous oceanographer is Jacques Cousteau (jock koo-**stow**). He was born in France in 1910. Cousteau has made people more aware of the ocean and its resources. He has said that if we wish to survive on land, we must learn about the ocean.

CHAPTER 2 OCEAN MOVEMENTS

1 CURRENTS

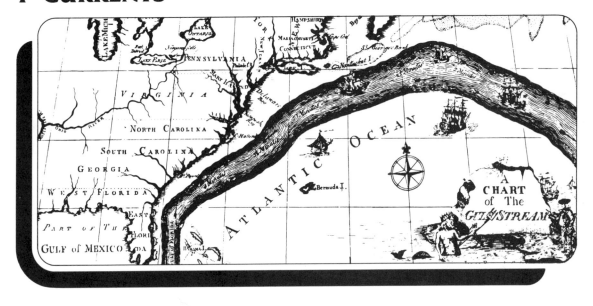

Benjamin Franklin was a great leader and inventor. He was also an oceanographer. Franklin realized that American ships crossed the Atlantic Ocean faster than English ships. His cousin, a ship captain, told Franklin there was a place in the ocean where the water moved swiftly, like a river. American ships sailed with this fast-moving water toward England. Franklin made a map to show where the fast-moving water was located. He called the moving water the Gulf Stream.

When you finish this lesson, you should be able to:

○ Tell the name given to ocean water that moves in a certain direction.

○ Explain how winds and the sun cause this movement of water.

○ Name the winds that cause this movement.

Current: Water that moves in a certain direction.

The Gulf Stream is a **current** (**kur**-rent). A *current* is water that moves in a certain direction. Look at the map on page 17. In what direction does the Gulf Stream move?

Right now, as you are reading your book, the earth is spinning. You don't feel the spinning because the movement is slow. However, the spinning causes the air around the earth to move. Moving air creates wind. The wind moves over the ocean surface pushing against the water. The water moves with the wind.

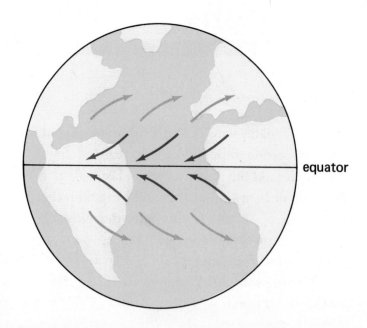

equator

As they blow toward the equator, the winds move from the east to the west. These winds are called **trade winds**. Look at the diagram at the bottom of page 18. Find the equator. Find the red arrows that show the blowing *trade winds*. Winds that blow away from the equator move from west to east. These winds are called **westerlies** (**west**-tur-lees). Find the blue arrows that show the blowing *westerlies*. As the trade winds and westerlies blow, they push the ocean water in the same direction. A giant, circling current results.

Look at the diagram below. The thick red arrows show the circling currents. The thin blue arrows show the winds that cause the currents. Find the numbers *1* and *2*. They show the part of the current in the Atlantic Ocean called the Gulf Stream. The numbers *3* and *4* show a current in the Pacific Ocean called the California current. Why do you think it was given that name?

Trade winds: Winds that blow from east to west toward the equator.

Westerlies: Winds that blow from west to east away from the equator.

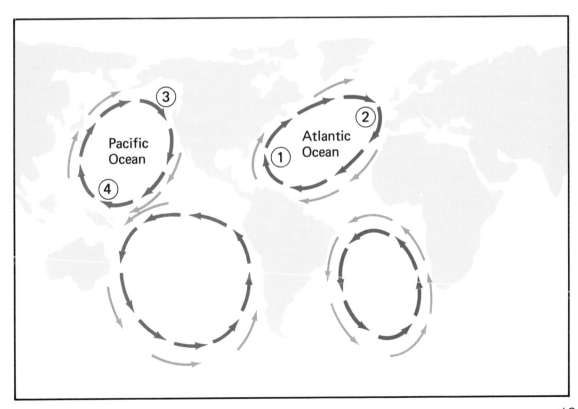

The currents you just read about are on the ocean surface. Other currents are below the surface. They are caused by the sun. The heat from the sun warms the ocean waters. The sun does not evenly heat all the ocean water. At the equator, ocean water is warm. Where do you think ocean water is cold?

Cold water sinks. The cold water at the North and South Poles sinks to the ocean bottom. The cold water slowly moves toward the equator. Warm water near the equator moves toward the poles to replace the sinking cold water. The movement of the cold and warm water causes deep currents. The currents circle between the poles and the equator.

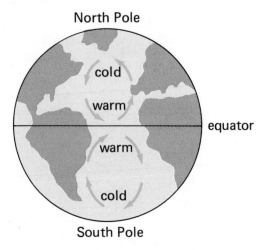

You know the amount of salt in ocean water is not the same all over. How does the sun's heat cause the water in some places to be saltier? The more salt in the water, the heavier the water is. Heavy water sinks to the ocean bottom. When it meets less salty water, the less salty water moves over it. A circling current forms. For example, the waters of the Mediterranean Sea are saltier than the Atlantic Ocean. Where these two bodies of water meet there is a deep current. The saltier, heavy water moves along the ocean bottom. The less salty water moves over the heavier water into the Mediterranean Sea.

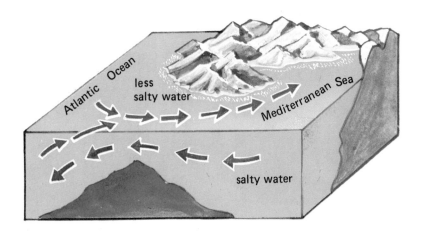

less salty water

Atlantic Ocean

Mediterranean Sea

salty water

MAIN IDEAS

Currents on the ocean's surface are due to winds caused by the spinning of the earth. Trade winds and westerlies are the names of two of these winds. Deep ocean currents are caused by the uneven heating of ocean water by the sun. This uneven heating causes the movement of cold and warm water, and salty and less salty water.

QUESTIONS

Write your answers on a sheet of paper.

1. What is a current? Name a strong current in the Atlantic Ocean.
2. What are the names of the winds that cause currents on the ocean surface?
3. How do these winds cause currents?
4. The oceans on the earth are unevenly heated by the sun. Explain why this causes deep ocean currents.
5. How does the amount of salt in the ocean cause deep currents?

2 WAVES

Are you a wave watcher? Do you know any wave watchers? Surfers are. They watch waves that roll in toward the beach. What do you think they look for?

When you finish this lesson, you should be able to:

○ Tell how wind causes waves.

○ Draw and label a wave.

○ Explain how waves change the shore.

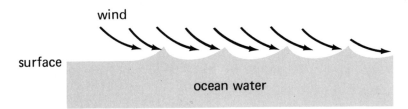

wind

surface

ocean water

In the last lesson you learned how wind causes currents. Wind also causes waves. As wind moves over the water, it pushes against the surface. This movement causes part of the water to rise. The wind then pushes on the raised water and a wave is created. As the wind continues to blow, more waves are made.

What does a wave look like? A wave has two parts. The highest point of the wave is called the **crest**. The lowest point is called the **trough (troff)**. The height of a wave is the distance from its *crest* to its *trough*. The length of a wave is the distance from its crest to the crest of the next wave. Waves move in the same direction as the wind. The size of a wave depends on the strength of the wind.

Crest: The highest point of a wave.

Trough: The lowest point of a wave.

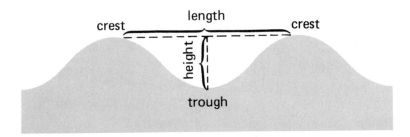

length

crest

crest

height

trough

Breaker: A wave in which the crest has tumbled forward.

As a wave moves into shallow water near the shore, its trough rubs against the ocean bottom. The rubbing causes the trough to slow down. However, the crest still moves quickly. It gets higher and leans forward. The crest may lean so far forward that it tumbles over, forming a white foam. The wave is then called a **breaker**. Have you ever seen a *breaker*? What do you think happens when a breaker hits the shore?

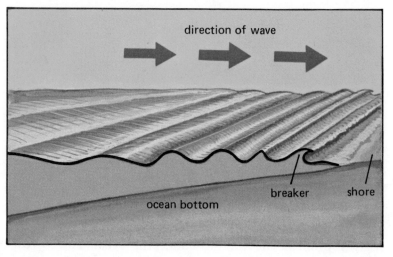

direction of wave

ocean bottom   breaker   shore

ACTIVITY

Materials
2 blocks of wood
long tray
milk container
sand
water

A. Place one block of wood under one end of the tray so that the tray is on a slope.

B. Fill that end of the tray with sand. Shape the sand into a sloping beach.

C. Fill your milk container with water. Pour the water into the tray at the other end. Stop pouring when the level of the water meets the beach.

D. Hold the other block of wood in the water at the end of the tray opposite the beach.

E. Gently push the wood toward the beach and then back 15 times, waiting a few seconds each time.

1. What formed in the water?

2. What happened to the beach?

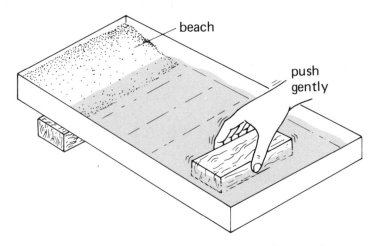

beach

push gently

The motion of your hand and the wood caused waves in the water. The waves hit against the sand and pulled some sand into the water.

After a wave breaks against the beach, the wave moves back into the ocean. It moves under the waves coming in. As the wave moves back into the ocean, it carries sand from the beach. Each time a wave breaks, the beach is reshaped. Over a long period of time, waves can reshape a beach area.

Not all shores are beaches. Waves also hit against shores of rocks and mountains. The waves chip away parts of the mountains and break up the rocks. Over a long time, the rocks become tiny grains of sand and a beach can form.

Wind causes waves. The highest point of a wave is its crest. The lowest point is its trough. When the crest of a wave tumbles into foam, a breaker forms. Breakers carry sand away from the beach. Waves also chip away mountains, break up rocks, and form new beaches.

QUESTIONS

Write your answers on a sheet of paper.

1. How does wind form waves?

2. Draw two waves. Label their crests and troughs.

3. How do waves change a beach?

4. What happens when waves hit mountains and rocks?

SOMETHING EXTRA

Can you imagine a wave as high as the first floor of your school building? The largest wave ever recorded was 64 m (210 ft) high. The wave was seen off the coast of Siberia on October 6, 1737.

Giant waves are usually caused by hurricanes or underwater earthquakes. These giant waves are called **tsunami** (soo-**nahm**-mees). In Japanese, *tsunami* means storm wave.

3 TIDES

Look at the two pictures above. They show the same place. What is different? When you finish this lesson, you should be able to:

○ Tell the name given to the rise and fall of ocean water.

○ Explain what causes the ocean water to rise and fall.

○ Tell when these changes occur.

The pictures show the Bay of Fundy. The Bay of Fundy is along the shore of New Brunswick, Canada. In one picture the bay is filled with water. In the other picture, it is not.

**Tides: The rise and
fall of ocean water.**

The rise and fall of ocean water is called **tides.** When
the water is at its highest level, we say there is a high
tide. Which picture on page 27 shows the Bay of Fundy
at high tide? When the water is at its lowest level, there
is a low tide. Which picture shows the Bay of Fundy at
low tide?

Tides occur along every ocean coast. The height of the
tides differs from one place to another. Tides are caused
by the pull of the moon on the earth. Look at the diagram. The letter *A* represents the earth. The letters *B*, *C*,
D, and *E* represent the oceans on the earth. The moon
pulls on the ocean water at *B*, causing the water to bulge.
The bulge creates a high tide on that side of the earth.
The moon also pulls on the solid earth, shown as *A*. The
moon pulls more on *A* than *C*, causing another bulge.
This bulge creates a high tide on the opposite side of the
earth. The water at *D* and *E* flattens and low tides occur
there. Because of the earth's spinning, the tides at *B*, *C*,
D, and *E* will change. When the tides become high at *D*
and *E*, there will be low tides at *B* and *C*.

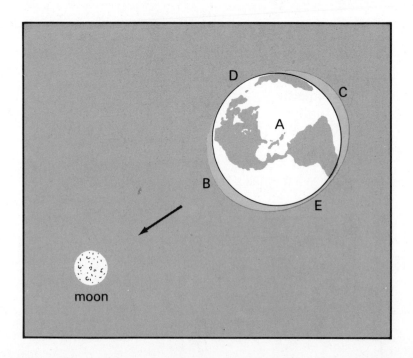

A. The chart below gives the height of the water every hour in Boston Harbor for January 1.

B. Using the information on the chart, answer these questions.

   1. At what time did the first low tide occur?

   2. At what time did the first high tide occur?

   3. How many hours passed between the first low tide and the first high tide?

   4. At what time did the second low tide occur? the second high tide?

   5. How many hours passed between the first and the second high tides? the first and the second low tides?

Materials
none

Height of Water in Boston Harbor on January 1st

time	1 A.M.	2 A.M.	3 A.M.	4 A.M.	5 A.M.	6 A.M.	7 A.M.	8 A.M.	9 A.M.	10 A.M.	11 A.M.	12 noon
height of water (meters)	2.0	1.7	1.6	1.9	2.4	2.9	3.4	3.8	4.0	3.7	3.3	2.7
	1 P.M.	2 P.M.	3 P.M.	4 P.M.	5 P.M.	6 P.M.	7 P.M.	8 P.M.	9 P.M.	10 P.M.	11 P.M.	12 mid-night
height of water (meters)	2.2	1.6	1.2	1.3	1.6	2.1	2.6	4.6	3.4	3.5	3.2	2.8

The tides change from high to low about every six hours. In a twenty-four hour period there are two high tides and two low tides. If you know when the last high tide occurred, you can predict when the next one will occur. For example, if the last high tide was at 10:00 P.M., at what time will the next high tide occur?

There are certain times when the tides are very high and very low. These tides occur when the sun, earth, and moon form a straight line in space. At this time, both the sun and the moon pull on the earth. As a result, high tides are higher than usual, and low tides are lower than usual. This only occurs twice a month. These very high and very low tides are called **spring tides**.

When the earth, moon and sun are at right angles to each other, low tides are not very low. High tides are not very high. The tides are not as great because the pull of the sun decreases the moon's pull on the earth. These are called **neap tides (neep)**. The diagrams show the positions of the earth, moon, and sun when *spring tides* and *neap tides* occur. Look at the positions of the earth, moon, and sun in each diagram. The arrows show the direction of the moon's pull and the sun's pull.

Spring tides: Very high and very low tides.

Neap tides: Low tides that are not very low; high tides that are not very high.

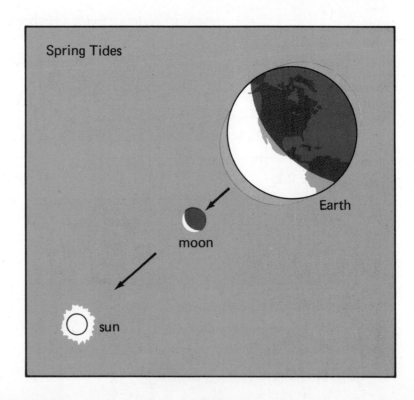

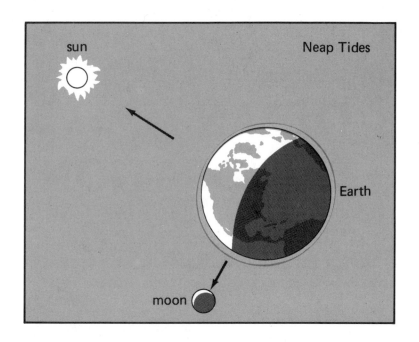

sun

Neap Tides

Earth

moon

Tides are caused by the pull of the moon on the earth. Sometimes the sun affects the tides too. Tides are called high, low, spring, and neap.

QUESTIONS

Write your answers on a sheet of paper.

1. What are tides?
2. Explain how the moon causes tides on earth. You may draw a diagram as part of your answer.
3. A high tide occurred in New York at 2:00 A.M. When will the next low tide occur? the next high tide?
4. What are spring and neap tides? What causes these tides?

CHAPTER

OCEAN EXPLORATION

1 OCEAN RESOURCES

Do you like cookies? What is your favorite kind? Would you like to eat a cookie made with food from the ocean? How do you think it would taste?

When you finish this lesson, you should be able to:

○ Name four resources we get from the ocean.

○ Tell how we get these resources.

The ocean is a rich source of food. However, only 10 percent of our food supply comes from the ocean. What foods from the ocean have you eaten?

On land, people have learned to farm to supply the food they need. New crops are grown each year and new animals raised to replace what has been used. People hunt for food in the ocean. They take food from the ocean but do not replace it. Scientists believe we can learn to farm in the ocean. We can grow new ocean plants or crops each year and raise ocean animals. Ocean farming would increase the amount of food we get from the ocean. Also, we would be able to replace the food we take from the ocean. Ocean farming would not be easy. What problems can you think of?

Ocean water contains many materials also found on land. These materials are dissolved in the water. You have learned about a dissolved salt. Can you name it? Look at the drawing. The words you see are names of materials dissolved in ocean water. The drawing also shows how the materials may be used. It is very expensive to get some of these materials out of the water. However, as we use up the supplies of these materials from the land, the ocean will be our only source.

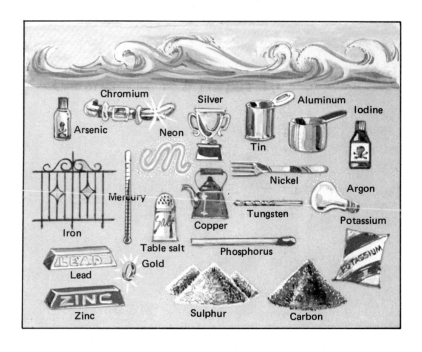

Fossil fuels: Fuels formed from remains of plants and animals.

Petroleum: A fossil fuel.

Natural gas: A fossil fuel.

The largest supply of **fossil fuels** (**foss**-sil **few**-ells) on earth may lie under the ocean bottom. *Fossil fuels* are formed from the remains of plants and animals that lived very long ago. These remains settled on the ocean bottom and were covered with layers of other sediment. The layers of sediment pushed down on the remains. After millions of years the remains changed to a liquid called **petroleum** (peh-**troll**-lee-um). *Petroleum* is a fossil fuel found under the ocean bottom. It is used to make gasoline and heating oil. Another fossil fuel is **natural gas**. Natural gas also is used to heat homes. *Natural gas* and petroleum are usually found together.

The equipment shown in the picture is used to drill under the ocean bottom to get fossil fuels from the ocean. It is difficult and expensive to drill for these fuels. However, when the supply from the land is used up, the ocean may be the only source of fossil fuels. There is a limited amount of fuels in the ocean as well. We will

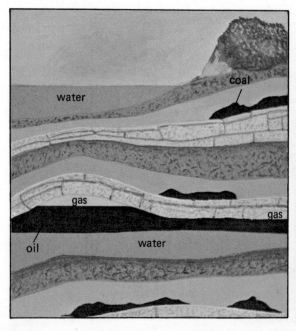

soon have to find other materials to do the job of fuels. Can you think of any?

In some parts of the world there is a shortage of fresh water. Fresh water is needed to grow crops. Ocean water can be used if the salt is taken out.

A. Study the diagram. Then answer these questions.

1. What is being done to the salt water?

2. What happens to water when it is heated?

3. Where will the evaporated water go?

4. What happens to the evaporated water in the tube when it is cooled by the ice?

5. What will happen to the salt?

Materials
none

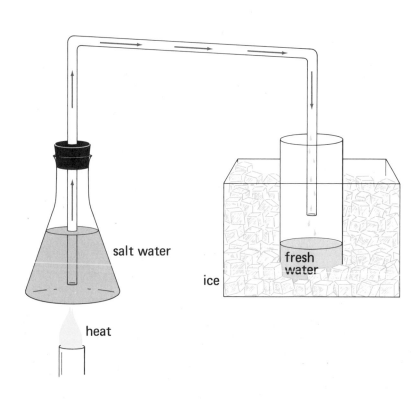

salt water

ice

fresh water

heat

Desalination: The process of removing salt from ocean water.

The process of removing salt from ocean water is called **desalination** (dee-sal-lin-**nay**-shun). Ocean water can be *desalinated* by heating it until the water evaporates. The evaporated water is then cooled until it becomes a liquid again. The salt is removed and the water is fresh. The process of desalination of ocean water is carried out in desalination plants. Salt water is pumped from the ocean to the plants and placed in large tanks. The water in the tanks is heated, evaporated, and changed to a liquid again.

MAIN IDEAS

The ocean is rich in resources. We use only a small amount of the food we can get from the ocean. We may be able to increase the amount of food through ocean farming. Materials dissolved in ocean water can be made into useful products. The ocean has the largest supply of fossil fuels on earth. Desalination can be used to get fresh water from salty ocean water.

QUESTIONS

Write your answers on a sheet of paper.

1. What are four resources we can get from the ocean?
2. How would ocean farming help us?
3. Why is it difficult to use the materials dissolved in ocean water?
4. What is desalination? Explain how it is done and why.

2 OCEAN LIFE

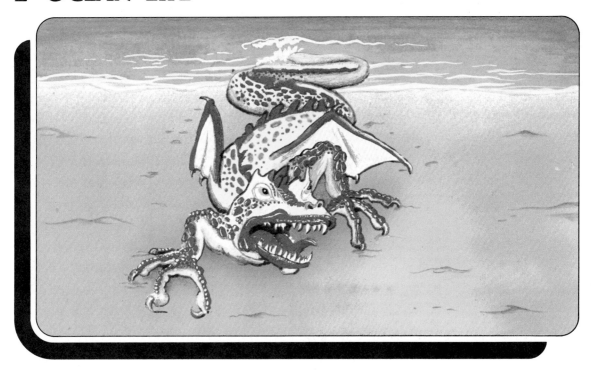

There are many tales about huge monsters living in the deep waters of the ocean. About 60 million years ago, large ocean animals did live in the ocean. Today there are animals in the ocean larger than some that lived long ago. However, we don't think of them as monsters. They are some of the interesting animals living in the ocean.

When you finish this lesson, you should be able to:

○ Tell where living things are found in the ocean.

○ Name and describe the living things found in each part of the ocean.

○ Explain how life in the ocean is like a pyramid.

There are three places in the ocean where life is found: on the surface, on the bottom near the shores, and just below the surface.

Plankton: Tiny plants and animals on the ocean surface.

Copepods: Tiny shrimp like animals.

Thousands of tiny plants and animals float on the surface of the ocean. They are called **plankton** (**plank**-ton). *Plankton* are so tiny, they cannot be seen with the naked eye. Plankton live on the ocean surface, where there is sunlight, rather than on the ocean bottom. Tiny shrimp-like animals called **copepods** (**koe**-peh-pods) eat plankton. *Copepods* are as small as the head of a pin.

On the ocean bottom near the shore, there are many plants and animals. Here, sunlight reaches the bottom and many plants are able to grow. Why do you think there is little plant growth in the deeper parts of the ocean?

A great variety of animals live in the water near the shore. Crabs, lobsters, and shrimps move along the ocean bottom looking for food. Some fish swim along the bottom too. They all eat plankton that fall from the surface. They also eat parts of other ocean animals. The starfish uses its long arms to pry open clams and scallops. The **sea anemone** (ah-**nem**-oh-nee) sits on the ocean bottom waiting for a fish to touch its poisonous arms. The *sea anemone,* shown in the picture on the right, looks more like a plant than an animal.

Sea anemone: An ocean animal.

Most fish live in the deeper water, just below the ocean surface. Fish eat other fish to stay alive. Large fish eat smaller ones, which eat smaller ones, which eat still smaller ones. The small fish eat copepods and plankton. For example, sharks may eat codfish, which eat herring, which eat copepods, which eat plankton. This eating pattern is called a **food chain**. A *food chain* can be described as who-eats-whom.

Food chain: A pattern of who-eats-whom.

Life in the ocean is like a pyramid. On the bottom of the pyramid are plankton. Each animal feeds on the plants and animals below it on the pyramid. At the top of the pyramid is the largest ocean animal, the whale.

In the ocean there is no place for a fish to hide from another. Therefore, many fish have coloring to protect them. From above, ocean water looks blue. Many fish are blue on top. From below, the water looks white and many fish have white bellies. The sting ray is a fish whose color matches the ocean bottom where it lives. Look at the picture on the next page. Can you find the sting ray buried in the sand?

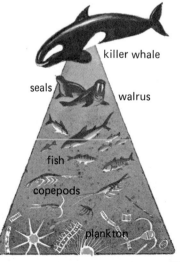

killer whale
seals
walrus
fish
copepods
plankton

Life in the ocean is found on the surface, on the bottom near the shores, and just below the surface. Plankton are tiny plants and animals that float on the surface. Animals on the bottom include crabs, starfish, and sea anemones. Fish swim just below the surface. Life in the ocean is like a pyramid.

QUESTIONS

Write your answers on a sheet of paper.

1. Name the three places in the ocean where life is found.
2. What are plankton? What are copepods?
3. Name three animals that live near the shore on the ocean bottom.
4. Tell how the arms of the starfish and sea anemone help them get food.
5. Why is life in the ocean like a pyramid? Which living things are at the bottom, the middle, and the top of the pyramid?

3 THE OCEAN IN DANGER

NO
SWIMMING ALLOWED
WATER POLLUTED
NO LIFE GUARD ON DUTY

Do you live near the ocean? Have you ever gone swimming in the ocean? Imagine it is a hot summer day. When you get to the ocean beach, you see a sign like the one shown above. How would you feel? Why do you think the sign is there?

When you finish this lesson, you should be able to:

○ Tell the word that means the adding of harmful materials to the ocean.

○ Explain why these materials are harmful.

○ Tell how adding these materials to the ocean can be prevented.

○ Explain why the blue whale is in danger.

The ocean beach shown is unfit for swimming because of **pollution** (poe-**loo**-shun). *Pollution* is the adding of harmful materials to something. This lesson is about polluting the ocean.

Pollution: The adding of harmful materials to the ocean.

41

Sewage: Waste materials carried by sewers and drains.

Pesticides: Chemicals sprayed on crops.

Pollution of the ocean is often caused by the dumping of **sewage** (**sue**-ij) in the water. *Sewage* is waste material carried by sewers and drains. Sewage contains germs that cause disease in ocean plants and animals. To prevent pollution, many cities have sewage treatment plants like the one shown. At these plants, the harmful materials are removed from the sewage.

Pollution can also be caused by chemicals in the water. Some chemicals are carried to the ocean by rivers. For example, **pesticides** (**pes**-tih-sides), chemicals sprayed on crops, run off the land into rivers. The *pesticides* are carried to the ocean. They are harmful to the living things there. What do you think happens to the plants and animals as a result? To prevent this pollution, laws have been passed to limit the amount and kind of chemicals used for spraying crops.

Another cause of pollution in the ocean occurs when oil leaks or spills from ships carrying it. It is very difficult to get the oil out of the water.

A. Fill your pan with water.

B. Pour some oil in the water.

    1. Did the oil mix with the water?

C. Try to remove the oil from the water with a spoon, the cotton, and the paper.

    2. Were you able to get the oil out of the water?

Materials
cotton
oil
pan
paper
spoon
water

Oil and water do not mix. Oil floats on the water's surface and is hard to remove. Waves and currents cause the oil to spread out and move toward the shore. Oil spills kill the plants and animals in the ocean and on the beach. Look at the picture of the bird. Its feathers are covered with oil. What do you think this does to the bird?

Hay is often used to clear oil from a beach. The hay soaks up the oil. In the ocean, chemicals are used to bring pools of oil together. Then the oil is sucked up with powerful hoses.

Some sea animals are in danger for a reason other than pollution. Blue whales are in danger of becoming **extinct** (ex - **stinkt**). An animal is *extinct* when there aren't any left. Blue whales have been hunted for many years. They are hunted for their meat, bones, and teeth. The graph below shows the number of blue whales killed since 1930. How many were killed in 1930? in 1970? The number of whales killed each year has decreased. There are two reasons. Because so many were killed between 1930 and 1940, there were simply fewer left to be killed later. Also, it is now against the law for American and European fisherman to hunt blue whales.

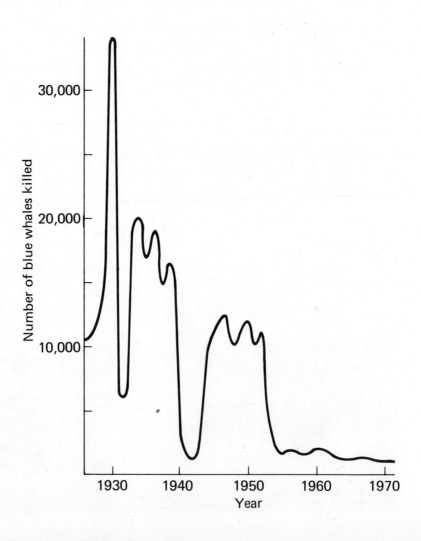

Pollution of the ocean is caused by sewage, chemicals, and oil spills. We have tried ways to prevent pollution of the ocean. Some sea animals are in danger for a reason other than pollution. The blue whale is in danger of becoming extinct. We have passed a law to prevent the killing of blue whales.

QUESTIONS

Write your answers on a sheet of paper.

1. What is the word that means the adding of harmful materials to the ocean?
2. Explain why the following materials are harmful when added to the ocean: a. sewage, b. chemicals such as pesticides, c. oil.
3. How can the adding of sewage and pesticides to the ocean be prevented?
4. Why is the blue whale in danger of extinction?

SOMETHING EXTRA

Have you ever gone fishing? Many people fish as a career. They catch over 130 billion tons of fish each year. The fish are used as food for humans and animals. Other useful products can be made from fish. For example, whale bones are used in making jewelry. Most people who fish as a career live near the ocean. Boston and New York were among the earliest fishing ports in this country.

4 OCEAN EXPLORATION

Have you ever swum underwater? Were you able to breathe? Were you able to see? How long could you stay underwater?

When you finish this lesson, you should be able to:

○ Describe two pieces of equipment people use underwater.

○ Tell how oceanographers use sound to make a picture of the ocean bottom.

○ Explain how oceanographers find out about sediments.

Without air from special equipment you could not stay underwater very long. At one time, divers got air through hoses attached to their ship. However, the hoses would often tangle and break.

In 1943, the **aqualung** (ak-wa-lung) was invented. The *aqualung* is an air tank worn on the diver's back with a hose from the tank to the diver's mouth. The aqualung allows divers to explore underwater for long periods of time. Look at the picture of the divers on page 46. Can you locate the parts of the aqualung? What do divers wear to safely open their eyes and see underwater?

Even with an aqualung and face mask, a diver can only swim to a certain depth. After a depth of more than 133 m (437 ft), the water presses against the diver so much that it can crush the diver. In order to explore greater depths, bathyscaphes (**bath**-ee-scafs) were invented. A *bathyscaphe* is an underwater ship. It can carry people and equipment to a depth of 3,600 m (about 11,000 ft). The bathyscaphe in the picture is called Alvin. Can you find the name on the ship?

Aqualung: An air tank worn on a diver's back.

Bathyscaphe: An underwater ship.

Echo sounder: An instrument that sends out sounds that hit the ocean bottom.

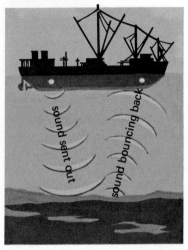

sound sent out

sound bouncing back

In the first lesson in this unit you learned about the ocean bottom. An **echo sounder** is used to find out where the high and low places are on the bottom. The *echo sounder* on a ship sends out sounds. The sounds travel through the water until they hit the bottom. Then the sounds bounce back to the ship. The time it takes for the sound to hit the ocean bottom and return to the ship is measured. Oceanographers can figure out how far the sound traveled if they know how long it took. Therefore, they know how far down the bottom is. A picture, like the one shown below, is made by the echo sounder. The picture shows the high and low places on the ocean bottom. Oceanographers found out about the mid-ocean ridge by using an echo sounder.

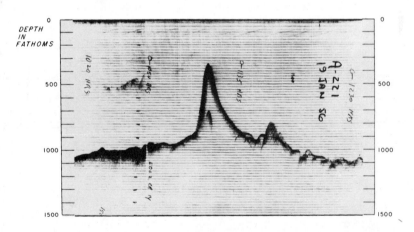

You have also learned about sediments on the ocean bottom. To find out about these sediments, a long hollow tube is lowered from a ship and drilled into the ocean bottom. The hollow part of the tube fills with sediment. The tube is brought back up to the ship and sliced in half lengthwise. Then oceanographers study the layers of sediment in the tube.

To find out about the underwater world, divers and oceanographers use special equipment. The aqualung supplies air to divers exploring underwater. The bathyscaphe carries people and equipment to the great depths of the ocean. An echo sounder is used to make a picture of the ocean bottom. To find out about sediments, a hollow tube is drilled into the ocean bottom. When the tube is removed, the sediments in the tube are studied.

QUESTIONS

Write your answers on a sheet of paper.

1. What is an aqualung?
2. What is a bathyscaphe? Why is it used?
3. How is sound used to make a picture of the ocean bottom?
4. How do oceanographers find out about sediments on the ocean bottom?

49

UNIT SUMMARY

The ocean bottom has three main parts: the continental shelf, continental slope, and ocean floor. The ocean floor consists of the abyssal plain and mid-ocean ridge. The ocean floor is believed to be spreading at the mid-ocean ridge. Ocean water is constantly moving due to currents, waves, and tides. The oceans provide resources such as food, fuels, and fresh water. The oceans contain many kinds of plants and animals. People have invented equipment for ocean exploration. The resources and life in the ocean are in danger because of pollution. We have ways of preventing pollution.

CHECK YOURSELF

Write your answers on a sheet of paper.
1. Match the words on the left with the phrases on the right.

a. continental shelf	a person who studies the ocean
b. submarine canyon	deep ocean valley
c. ocean floor	a salt
d. sediments	part of the continent covered by ocean
e. continental slope	covers most of the ocean bottom
f. sodium chloride	materials that settle in water
g. oceanographer	land in ocean that plunges sharply
h. trenches	groove cut in the continental shelf and slope

2. The abyssal plain and mid-ocean ridge are parts of the ocean floor. Explain how they are different.

3. Why is ocean water salty?
4. Why is the Atlantic Ocean getting wider? What is happening to the Pacific Ocean?
5. Explain how trade winds and westerlies cause currents.
6. What causes currents below the ocean's surface?
7. What causes surface waves? Describe the parts of a wave.
8. Explain why tides occur. In what position are the earth, moon, and sun when spring tides occur? when neap tides occur?
9. Why is the ocean an important resource?
10. What are fossil fuels? Name two.
11. What is desalination?
12. Name an animal that lives in each of the following parts of the ocean: on the surface, on the bottom near the shores, just below the surface.
13. List three causes of ocean pollution.
14. Tell why the following are important to oceanographers: aqualung, bathyscaphe, and echo sounder.

PROJECTS

1. You and your classmates should each select an ocean plant or animal to study. It may be one you read about in this unit or others you would like to find out more about. Library books about plants and animals will help you get information. Write a report. Make a papier-mâché model of the plants and animals. Hang the models around the classroom to make an ocean world aquarium. Give other classes a tour of your ocean aquarium. Tell them about each plant and animal.
2. Seafood is called "brain food." Find out why. Health and diet books can be helpful. For two weeks, keep a list of the seafood you eat. Find out the amount of calories, protein, and minerals in each of the foods.

A lightning bolt pierces the air and tears through a huge tree in a forest. The tree sways and falls to the ground. A loud crashing sound is made by the falling tree. But no one is in the forest to hear the sound. Is there a sound if no one is there to hear it? Or is sound a thing that exists with or without people? What do you think?

This unit is about sound. You will find out how sounds are made, how sounds travel, and how sounds are different from each other.

UNIT

2 SOUND

CHAPTER 4

WHAT IS SOUND?

1 HOW ARE SOUNDS MADE?

Sit very quietly. Listen carefully. What sounds do you hear? Cover your ears. What happened to the sounds? Have you ever been someplace where there was no sound?

When you finish this lesson, you should be able to:

○ Tell the word that describes a quick back-and-forth movement.

○ Explain how sounds are made.

Materials
plastic ruler

A. Place the ruler on your desk as shown in the drawing.

B. With one hand hold down the end of the ruler on your desk.

C. With your other hand, press down on the free end of the ruler and then quickly let go.

1. What do you hear?

2. How does the ruler move?

D. Repeat step C. Stop the ruler's movement with your hand.

3. What happened to the sound when the ruler stopped moving?

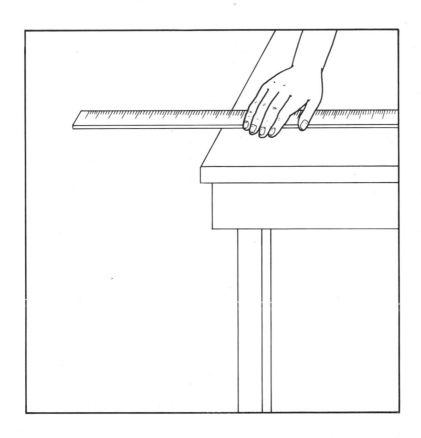

When an object or part of an object moves back and forth quickly we say it **vibrates** (**vi**-brayts). The ruler *vibrated* when you pressed down on the free end and then let go. A sound is made when something vibrates. When the ruler was vibrating, you heard a sound. When the ruler stopped vibrating, the sound stopped.

Look at the pictures. What sounds would you hear if you were there? What do you think is vibrating to cause the sounds?

The woodpecker's beak moves back and forth against the tree, causing a tapping sound. The jackhammer vibrates as it digs into the ground. When you speak or sing, your throat vibrates. Place your hand on your throat and hum. What do you feel?

MAIN IDEAS

Sounds are made when something vibrates. When the vibration stops, the sound stops.

QUESTIONS

Write your answers on a sheet of paper.

1. What word describes a quick back-and-forth movement?
2. Hold a rubber band as shown in the picture below. Pluck the rubber band with a finger from your other hand. Explain how a sound was made.

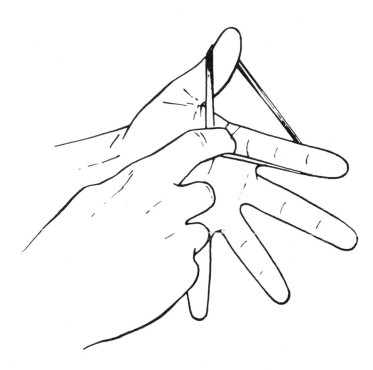

2 SOUND WAVES

The children are playing in the school yard. Suddenly, the school bell rings. The children stop playing and walk toward the school building. Why are the children able to hear the sound of the bell from different parts of the yard?

When you finish this lesson, you should be able to:

○ Tell the words that mean the crowding together and the spreading out of air particles.

○ Explain how sound travels.

All the children in the school yard could hear the bell because sound travels in all directions from its source. The source in this case was the bell. If a student seated in the middle of your classroom speaks loudly, can everyone in the room hear that student? Why?

ACTIVITY

Materials
Slinky

A. Stretch the Slinky across the floor. Hold one end while a classmate holds the other.

B. Quickly push your end of the Slinky in the direction of your classmate, then pull it back to its original position.

1. How did the Slinky move when you pushed and pulled it?

The coils of the Slinky bunched up and thinned out when you moved the Slinky. You only pushed and pulled once. However, the bunching and thinning traveled the whole length of the Slinky. If you pushed and pulled many times, the coils would have bunched up and thinned out many times. The motion of the Slinky is similar to the way sound travels.

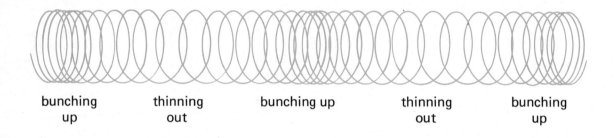

| bunching up | thinning out | bunching up | thinning out | bunching up |

Let's use a bell to describe how sound travels. The black dots you see near the bell in the drawing on page 61 represent air particles around the bell. When the bell is shaken, the clapper hits the bell's side. The side of the bell moves back and forth, or vibrates. As the side of the bell moves outward, it pushes on the air particles around it. This causes the air particles to crowd together, or bunch up. When you pushed on the Slinky the coils crowded together. The crowding together of air particles is called a **compression** (kom-**presh**-shun). A *compression* occurred where the coils crowded together.

Compression: The crowding together of air particles.

What happened to the coils when you pulled back? When the bell moves back, it leaves a space with fewer air particles. These air particles are spread apart. The spreading out of air particles is called a **rarefaction** (rare-eh-**fak**-shun). Sounds travel as a series of compressions followed by *rarefactions*. A series of compressions and rarefactions is called a **sound wave.** *Sound waves* travel in all directions from the source of the sound.

Rarefaction: The spreading out of air particles.

Sound wave: A series of compressions and rarefactions.

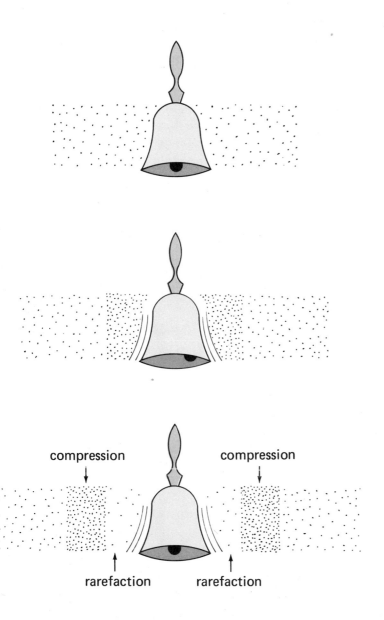

Vibrations cause a series of compressions and rarefactions. A series of compressions and rarefactions is called a sound wave. Sound waves travel in all directions from the source of the sound.

QUESTIONS

Write your answers on a sheet of paper.

1. What is the word that means the crowding together of air particles caused by a vibration? the spreading out of air particles?
2. Explain what happens to the air particles around a ringing telephone.

SOMETHING EXTRA

Before 1926 movies were called silent pictures. The movies did not have sound. The actors did not speak. They just moved their lips. What they would have said was shown as words on the screen. In 1926, the first talking movie was made. It was named *The Jazz Singer*. The sound came from a record that played while the movie was shown.

Scientists later found a way to put the sound on the film. Look at the edge of the piece of film in the picture. There are dark and light shadings there. The shadings are made by sound vibrations. The shadings are called a sound track.

3 THE SOUNDS OF MUSIC

The concert is about to begin. The musicians are tuning their instruments. What instruments do you see?

When you finish this lesson, you should be able to:

○ Name three types of musical instruments.

○ Tell how sound is made with these instruments.

In the above picture, you can see a guitar. A guitar is a **stringed instrument.** *Stringed instruments* have one or more strings. The strings vibrate when they are plucked, struck, or rubbed. What do you hear when the strings vibrate? How can the sound be stopped? Can you name other stringed instruments?

Stringed instrument: An instrument with one or more strings.

Another instrument shown in the picture on page 63 is a clarinet. A clarinet is a **wind instrument**. A *wind instrument* has a hollow column inside it, which is filled with air. The air column vibrates if someone blows into or across it. Most wind instruments are grouped as either woodwinds or brass. A clarinet is a woodwind. Woodwinds have a piece of wood in the mouthpiece called a **reed**.

Wind instrument: An instrument with an air column.

Reed: The piece of wood in the mouthpiece of a woodwind.

ACTIVITY

Materials
plastic straw
scissors

A. Flatten about 5 cm (2 in.) of one end of the straw.

B. Make a 2.5 cm (1 in.) cut along the folds made on each side of the straw.

C. Place the flattened end in your mouth and blow.

Blow until you hear a sound.

1. Did you feel anything as you blew into the straw?

2. What was vibrating as you blew?

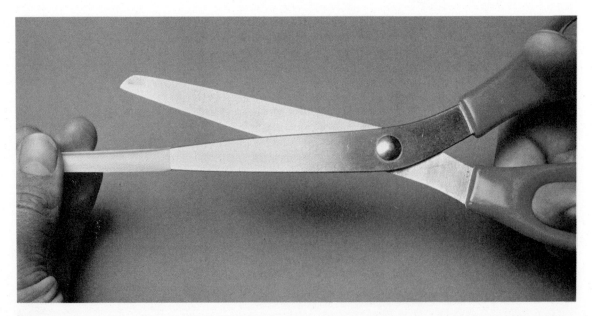

The flattened end of the straw is like the *reed* in a woodwind instrument. Blowing across a reed causes the reed to vibrate. The vibrating reed causes the air column in the instrument to vibrate and make a sound.

Brass wind instruments are made of the metal brass. Which instrument in the picture at the beginning of this lesson is brass? To play a trumpet, the musician presses his or her lips against the mouthpiece. When the musician blows out, his or her lips vibrate. The vibrating lips cause the air column in the trumpet to vibrate and make a sound.

Look at the picture below. Which instruments are woodwinds? Which are brass? Which are stringed instruments?

Can you think of an instrument that does not have strings or air columns? How about drums and cymbals? These are examples of **percussion instruments** (purr-**kush**-shun). *Percussion instruments* are made of solid materials or materials stretched over a container. A cymbal is made of a solid material. A drum has material stretched over a container. When a percussion instrument is hit, the solid or stretched material vibrates and makes a sound.

Percussion instrument: An instrument made of solid material or material stretched over a container.

IDEAS

Musical instruments make sounds in different ways. There are three types of musical instruments. Their sounds are made by a vibrating string, air column, or solid material.

QUESTIONS

Write your answers on a sheet of paper.

1. Name three types of musical instruments.
2. How are woodwinds and brass instruments different from each other?
3. Explain how sound is made by each of the following instruments and tell what type of instrument each is.
   a. trumpet   c. banjo
   b. bongo drum   d. clarinet

4 SOUND TRAVELS THROUGH DIFFERENT MATERIALS

Robert Boyle was a scientist who lived long ago. He wondered if sound could travel where there was no air. Boyle put a bell under a glass jar. He rang the bell and could hear it clearly. Using a pump, Boyle took the air out of the jar. He rang the bell again. What do you think he heard?

When you finish this lesson, you should be able to:

○ Tell the word that means a space without air.

○ Explain how sounds travel through different materials.

The second time Boyle rang the bell he could see it vibrating, but he did not hear it. Except for the bell, the inside of the glass was empty. There was no air. An empty space without air is called a **vacuum** (vak-youm). Sound cannot travel in a *vacuum*. A material through which sound can travel, such as air, is called a **medium**. Solids, liquids, and gases are *media*.

Vacuum: An empty space without air.

Medium: A material through which sound can travel.

A. With your finger, gently tap on one end of your desk. Listen carefully.

   1. How well did you hear the tapping?

B. Repeat step A but this time place your ear on your desk top.

   2. How well did you hear the tapping?

   3. How did the sound get to your ear?

Materials
none

Stethoscope: An
instrument used to
hear heartbeats.

The wood on your desk is a good medium for sound. When you tapped on your desk, sound waves traveled through the wood to your ear. Wood is a solid. Solids carry sounds very well. Long ago, Native Americans put their ears to the ground to find out if buffalo were near. Why do you think that worked?

Has your doctor ever listened to your heartbeat with a **stethoscope** (steth-oh-scope)? A *stethoscope* is an instrument through which sound travels very well. When the round disc on the end of the stethoscope is placed on your chest, the disc vibrates as your heart beats. The vibrations send sound waves through the air in the rubber tubes to the doctor's ears. The sound of your heartbeat is heard by the doctor. The air in the tubes contains many gases. Gases are a medium for sound.

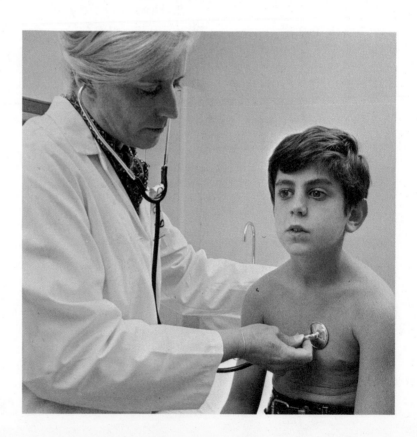

Liquids, such as water, are also good media for sound. People swimming under water can hear oncoming motor boats very well. The vibrations from the motor send sound waves through the water to the swimmer's ears.

Sounds travel better through solids than through liquids, and travel better through liquids than through gases.

MAIN IDEAS

Sounds cannot travel in a vacuum. Sounds can travel through solids, liquids, and gases.

QUESTIONS

Write your answers on a sheet of paper.

1. What is the word that means an empty space without air?
2. Explain how the boy in the picture below can hear what his friend is whispering into the paper cup telephone.

CHAPTER 5 HOW SOUNDS ARE DIFFERENT

1 THE SPEED OF SOUND

Imagine you are watching a track meet. The runners are set. The starter shouts "On your mark! Get set." You see a flash of light from the starter's gun. The runners are off. Then you hear the sound of the gun. Why do you think you saw the light from the gun before you heard the sound?

When you finish this lesson, you should be able to:

○ Tell how fast sound travels in air.

○ Explain how the speed of sound depends on the medium through which it travels.

Materials
Slinky

A. Hold one end of the Slinky. Have a classmate hold the other end.

B. Move apart until the Slinky is stretched.

C. Quickly push your end of the Slinky in the direction of your classmate and pull it back to its original position. Watch the wave move along the spring.

D. Repeat step C except this time, as the wave moves, count how long it takes for the wave to reach your classmate. Count by saying, "one second, two seconds," and so on.

1. How long did it take the wave to travel to your partner?

E. Repeat step D two times. Each time push and pull the Slinky harder.

2. Did the wave move faster? slower? the same?

The Slinky wave took a few seconds to travel from one end to the other. The wave did not travel faster when you pushed harder. Sound waves take time to travel too. The speed of a sound wave in air is 344 m/sec (1130 ft/sec). All sounds travel at that speed in air no matter how the sounds are made.

Sounds travel at different speeds in different media. Look at the chart below. What is the speed of sound in water? in wood? in steel? Sounds travel faster in solids than in liquids. Sounds travel slowest in gases.

medium	speed of sound
air	344 m/sec (1130 ft/sec)
water	1463 m/sec (4760 ft/sec)
wood	3050 m/sec (10,000 ft/sec)
steel	5002 m/sec (16,400 ft/sec)

Lightning and thunder occur at the same time. However, light travels much faster than sound. The light reaches your eyes before the sound reaches your ears. Why do you think you could see the light from the starter's gun before you heard the sound?

Sounds travel at different speeds in different media. The speed of sound in air is 344 m/sec (1130 ft/sec). Sounds travel fastest in solids.

QUESTIONS

Write your answers on a sheet of paper.

1. If you sneeze, how fast will the sound of your sneeze travel? Will the speed increase if you sneeze harder?
2. Explain in what way the speed of sound is different in different media. Give examples of different media in your answer.

SOMETHING EXTRA

Sound travels at a speed of 344 m/sec (1130 ft/sec) in air. The speed of sound is important when scientists talk about the speed of an airplane. The speed of an airplane is described by a **Mach** (**moc**) number. *Mach* 1 means the airplane is traveling at the same speed as sound. Mach 2 means twice the speed of sound.

When an airplane travels faster than the speed of sound a **sonic boom** is heard. A *sonic boom* sounds like loud thunder.

An airplane that travels faster than sound is the SST, or supersonic transport. An SST is shown in the picture.

2 LOUD AND SOFT SOUNDS

Jack plays guitar in the school band. Every day he practices his tunes. Jack's sister is studying in the next room. She calls to him and says that his guitar playing is too loud. How can Jack soften the sound of his guitar?

When you finish this lesson, you should be able to:

○ Tell the word that means the loudness or softness of a sound.

○ Explain why sounds are loud or soft.

○ Tell how sounds are measured.

The sounds you hear differ in loudness and softness. The loudness or softness of a sound is called its **intensity** (in-**ten**-sit-tee). Sounds that are loud have a high *intensity*. Soft sounds have a low intensity.

Intensity: The loudness or softness of a sound.

Materials
plastic ruler

A. Place your ruler on your desk as shown in the drawing.

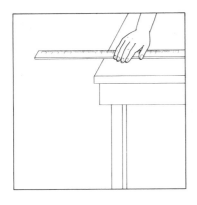

B. With one hand, hold down the end of the ruler on your desk. With your other hand gently push down on the free end and let go. Watch the ruler's movement. Listen to the sound.

C. Repeat step B except push down harder on the free end of the ruler.

1. Did the ruler vibrate more or less than the first time?

2. How was the sound different?

The loudness or softness of a sound depends on how strongly the object making the sound vibrates. Stronger vibrations make larger sound waves. Larger sound waves make more intense, or louder, sounds. The vibration of the ruler was stronger the second time you pushed the ruler. The sound was louder. You pushed harder to make a louder sound.

The more effort used to make a sound, the larger the sound wave and the louder the sound. What do you think would happen if you used less effort? Jack can lower the intensity of his guitar by plucking the strings more gently.

Decibels: Units of measurement of sound intensity.

The intensity of a sound can be measured with a sound-level meter. The first picture below shows a sound-level meter. Intensity is measured in units called **decibels** (**dess**-si-bells). The higher the *decibel* number the louder the sound. Look at the chart. It lists kinds of sounds and their decibel numbers. Which sound has the lowest intensity? Which sound has the highest intensity? What would the decibel number of your voice be if you answered those questions aloud?

Look at the picture on the next page. Using the chart, what do you think might be the decibel number for the sounds being made?

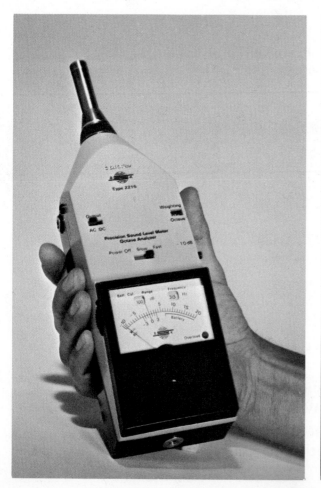

sound	number of decibels
whisper	15
automobile	45
conversation	65
heavy traffic	75
thunder	110
painful sounds	120
jet airplane	140

MAIN IDEAS

Sounds differ in intensity. The intensity of a sound depends on how strongly the object making the sound vibrates. The intensity of some sounds can be changed. The intensity of a sound can be measured.

QUESTIONS

Write your answers on a sheet of paper.

1. What is the word that means the loudness or softness of a sound?
2. What is the difference between the sound wave of a loud and a soft sound? How can a sound be made more intense? less intense?
3. What is the unit of measurement for sound intensity? What instrument is used to measure sound?

3 HIGH AND LOW SOUNDS

Look at the picture above. What sounds would you hear if you were standing there? How would the sounds be different from each other?

When you finish this lesson, you should be able to:

○ Tell the word that means the highness or lowness of a sound.

○ Explain how vibrations affect the highness or lowness of sounds.

○ Explain why we can or cannot hear certain sounds.

You have learned that sounds are caused by vibrations. The number of vibrations in one second can be counted. The number of vibrations made in one second is called **frequency** (**free**-kwen-see). We hear sounds that have a *frequency* of 20 to 20,000 vibrations per second.

Frequency: The number of vibrations made per second.

Materials
comb
index card

A. Hold the comb in one hand and the index card in the other.

B. Move the index card over the teeth of the comb as shown in the picture.

1. What did you hear?

2. What was vibrating?

C. Repeat step B three times, moving the card faster each time.

3. What happened to the sound?

You heard a sound when you moved the card over the teeth of the comb. The comb was vibrating. The comb vibrated faster when you moved the card quicker. The sound you heard was higher. The highness or lowness of a sound is called **pitch**. Low sounds have a low *pitch*. High sounds have a high pitch.

Pitch: The highness or lowness of a sound.

The pitch of a sound depends on how fast the object making the sound vibrates. An object vibrating quickly makes more vibrations in one second than an object vibrating slowly. We say the sound has a greater frequency. If the sound has a greater frequency, it has a higher pitch. The tuba and drum shown in the picture at the beginning of the lesson make low pitched sounds. What about the whistle, flute, and car?

Frequency also determines if you will hear a sound at all. Some people have dog whistles that their pet can hear but they cannot. A dog can hear sounds that vibrate more than 20,000 times a second. Sounds with a frequency greater than 20,000 vibrations per second are called **ultrasonic** (uhl-tra-**son**-ick) sounds. We cannot hear *ultrasonic* sounds.

Ultrasonic: Having a frequency greater than 20,000 vibrations per second.

Look at the chart on the next page. Which animals can hear very high pitched sounds? Which animal can hear sounds at a pitch less than 20 vibrations per second?

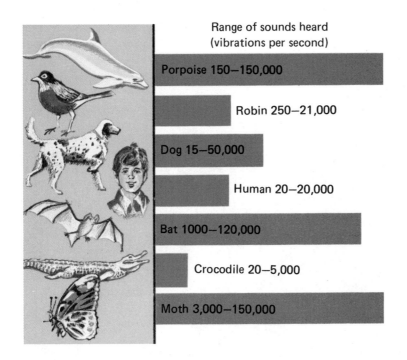

Range of sounds heard
(vibrations per second)

Porpoise 150—150,000

Robin 250—21,000

Dog 15—50,000

Human 20—20,000

Bat 1000—120,000

Crocodile 20—5,000

Moth 3,000—150,000

MAIN IDEAS

Sounds differ in pitch. The faster an object vibrates the higher its pitch. We cannot hear ultrasonic sounds. Some animals can.

QUESTIONS

Write your answers on a sheet of paper.

1. What is the word that means the highness or lowness of a sound?
2. How does frequency relate to the pitch of a sound?
3. What are ultrasonic sounds? Why can't we hear them? Name two animals that can.

4 CHANGING PITCH

Look closely at the picture of the guitar strings. How are they the same? How are they different?

When you finish this lesson, you should be able to:

○ List three things that affect the pitch of a vibrating string.

○ Tell how the pitch of a vibrating string can be changed.

○ Tell how the pitch of a wind instrument can be changed.

The strings of a guitar are different thicknesses. How do you think thickness affects the sound made by each string?

A. Stretch the rubber bands around the box as shown. They should be placed in order from thinnest to thickest.

B. Number each rubber band as shown. The thinnest band should be numbered *1*.

C. Starting with band 1, pluck each band once using the same amount of effort.

    1. Which band made the highest sound? the lowest sound?

2. Which band is the thinnest? the thickest?

D. Repeat step C. This time watch the bands closely as you pluck them.

    3. Which band vibrated fastest? slowest?

E. Pluck the thickest band once. Then hold the band about 2.5 cm (1 in.) from the edge of the shoebox and pluck it again.

    4. How did the sound change?

Materials
pencil
4 rubber bands of
  different thicknesses
shoe box

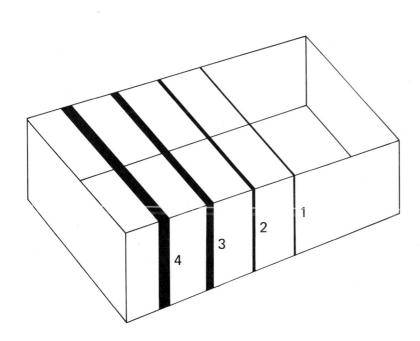

The strings on a guitar and the rubber bands on your box make sounds that have different pitches. One thing that determines the pitch of the strings is their thicknesses. The thin strings make high pitched sounds. The thick strings make low pitched sounds. The thin strings make more vibrations in one second. They have a greater frequency.

The pitch of a vibrating string also depends on the string's length. When you held part of the band, only the free part of the band could vibrate. It was as if you shortened the band. The sound you heard was higher. Shortening a string makes its pitch higher. What do you think happens if the string is longer?

Look at the girl in the picture. Many stringed instruments have pegs at one end. The strings are attached to the pegs. Turning the pegs loosens or tightens the strings. Loosening a string lowers its pitch. Tightening a string raises its pitch. The pitch of a vibrating string depends on how loose or tight the string is.

The boy in the picture is blowing air into the bottles. The air column in each bottle is different. When the boy blows into the air column above the water, the air vibrates. Remember how the pitch of your rubber band changed when it was shortened? When the air column in the bottles is shortened, the same thing happens. The pitch becomes higher. Which bottle would have the lowest pitch? What type of instruments have an air column? Some wind instruments have parts that can change the length of the air column. For example, a trombone has a slide. The slide moves in and out of the hollow tube, changing the length of the air column.

The pitch of a vibrating string depends on the string's length, thickness, and tightness. The pitch of a vibrating string can be changed. The higher the pitch, the more vibrations made per second. The pitch of an air column can be changed.

QUESTIONS

Write your answers on a sheet of paper.

1. List three things that affect the pitch of a vibrating string.
2. What are two ways you could change the pitch of the strings on a banjo?
3. How would the pitch of a trumpet change if the air column inside it were lengthened? shortened?
4. Look at the picture below. As the boy plays the guitar, he presses the string against the long narrow part of the guitar. Explain why that changes the pitch of the string.

CHAPTER  6 SOUNDS AROUND US

1 ECHOES

Before 1800, a scientist named Lazzaro Spallanzani wondered how bats could fly in total darkness and not bump into anything. He experimented and found out that when a bat's ears were covered, the bat bumped into things as it flew. What does this tell you about sound and a bat's ability to fly?

When you finish this lesson, you should be able to:

○ Tell what happens when a sound bounces off an object.

○ Explain why a bat can fly in total darkness.

○ Tell how bouncing sounds can be prevented.

Reflect: To bounce off an object.

Look at the picture below. The boy is playing ball against the wall. What will happen to the ball when it hits the wall? Sound bounces off objects in the same way a ball bounces off the wall. We say the sound is **reflected** (re-**flek**-ted). If the boy in the picture said his name aloud, the sound would be *reflected* from the wall.

When a sound is reflected from an object, an **echo** (**ek**-ko) is heard. An *echo* will only be heard if you are standing at least 16.8 m (55 ft) from the reflecting object. This allows time for the sound to hit the object and be reflected before the next sound you make is heard. Otherwise, the echo will not be heard as a separate sound. It will mix with other sounds being made. Sometimes, the sound is reflected from many objects and many echoes are heard.

When Lazzaro Spallanzani watched bats fly, he only heard the flapping of their wings. However, bats make other sounds as they fly. The sounds are ultrasonic. Why can't people hear bat sounds?

Echo: A sound reflected from an object.

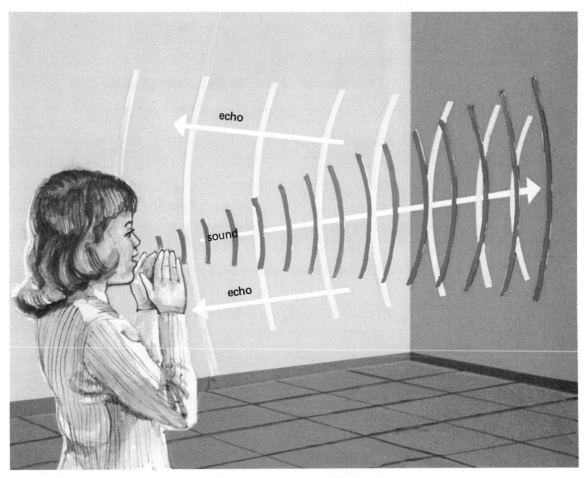

Bats are able to hear ultrasonic sounds. As a bat flies, it makes these sounds. The sounds are reflected from objects and echoes are heard by the bat. The bat can tell where the objects are when it hears the echoes. For this reason the bat can fly in darkness without bumping into things.

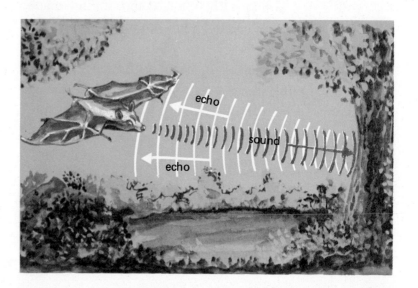

Echoes are helpful to a bat. However, echoes can be disturbing to people. Echo sounds can mix with other sounds and make these other sounds unclear. Probably there is a place in your school building where echoes occur. Do you know where? Echoes occur in large, empty rooms such as auditoriums.

Absorb: To take in.

There are ways to control echoes. Certain materials used on walls, ceilings, and floors stop sounds from being reflected. These materials **absorb** (ab-**sorb**), or take in, the sound. Soft materials such as cloth drapes and rugs *absorb* sound. Materials with tiny holes, such as cork, break up sound waves. The sound waves cannot be reflected. Ceiling tiles are often made of materials with tiny holes. People help absorb sounds too. When an auditorium is filled with people, echoes usually are not heard. Look at the picture on the next page. How can the room be changed to prevent echoes?

Sounds are reflected from objects. Sometimes an echo is heard when a sound is reflected. Bats make ultrasonic sounds that are reflected from objects and help them fly.

QUESTIONS

Write your answers on a sheet of paper.

1. What happens when a sound is reflected from an object that is at least 16.8 m (55 ft) away?
2. Why can a blindfolded bat fly without bumping into things? What would happen if the bat's ears were covered?
3. How can echoes be prevented in large, empty rooms?

2 SENDING SOUND MESSAGES

Two hundred years ago it took over three months to send a letter from Boston to San Francisco. Mail was sent by pony express or stagecoach. The mail was one of the only ways to send messages over long distances. Today, we have many ways of sending messages. We can even send sound messages to places that are far away.

When you finish this lesson, you should be able to:

○ Name and describe two parts of a telephone.

○ Explain how sounds are made by a telephone and a phonograph.

You probably have a telephone in your home. The sounds you make into the telephone are heard by the person at the other end. The person may be in the next house or very far away. How do you think the sounds get there? The actual sounds you make don't travel through telephone wires.

The part of the telephone you speak into is called the **transmitter** (trans-**mitt**-ter). Inside the *transmitter* is a metal disc. When you speak, the metal disc vibrates in the same pattern as your voice vibrations. This pattern is carried by the electricity in the telephone wires. The electricity travels through the wires to the telephone **receiver** (re-**see**-ver). The *receiver* is the part of the telephone through which you hear. At the receiver, the electricity causes another metal disc to vibrate. The original sound is then heard by the listener. The first telephone was invented in 1875 by Alexander Graham Bell.

Two years after the invention of the telephone, the first phonograph was invented by Thomas Edison. He is shown in the first picture on page 96.

Transmitter: The part of the telephone you speak into.

Receiver: The part of the telephone through which you hear.

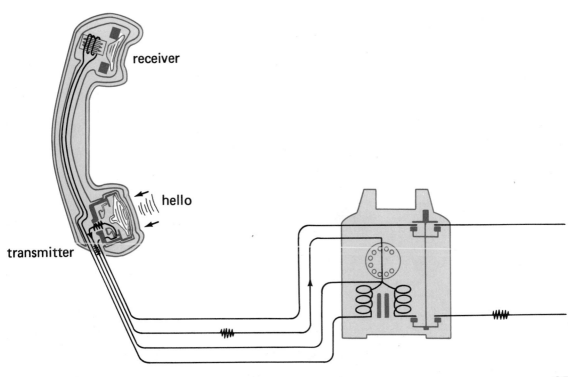

receiver

hello

transmitter

95

For Edison's phonograph, sounds were recorded on a record. The record was a cylinder with grooves on it. In the grooves was tin foil. The artist or singer spoke or sang into a horn. The vibrating horn caused a needle to vibrate. The vibrating needle moved through the grooves making a pattern on the tin foil. To play the record, it was placed on a phonograph. A needle on the phonograph moved through the grooves on the record. The pattern on the tin foil caused the needle to vibrate in the same pattern. These vibrations caused the phonograph speaker to vibrate in the pattern of the original sounds.

To make records today, we start with a flat, metal disc with a spiral groove cut in it. Sounds sent through a microphone cause a needle to move from side to side in the grooves. The needle cuts a pattern along the walls of the groove. The recording on the metal disc is transferred to a plastic record. The plastic record is placed on a record player. As the record spins, a needle moves through the grooves. The needle picks up the pattern of the vibrations that is cut into the grooves. The vibrations are changed back to sounds.

MAIN IDEAS

Sounds can be sent over long distances. A telephone changes sound so that it can pass through wires to a receiver. Sound vibrations cut a pattern in the grooves on a record. The record can then be played on a record player.

QUESTIONS

Write your answers on a sheet of paper.

1. Name and describe two parts of a telephone.
2. How are sounds sent over long distances by a telephone?
3. How are sounds recorded on a record and played on a phonograph?

SOMETHING EXTRA

Robert Moog is a scientist. He is also a musician. Moog invented a new kind of musical instrument. It is not a woodwind, stringed, or percussion instrument. It is a computer. The computer can make sounds like regular instruments. It also makes beeps, squeaks, and buzzes. The computer can play rock music as well as classical music. In 1968, an album of computer music was made. The album was named *Switched On Bach*.

UNIT SUMMARY

Sounds are made when something vibrates. When the vibration stops, the sound stops. Vibrations cause a series of compressions and rarefactions. A series of compressions followed by rarefactions is called a sound wave. Sound waves travel in all directions from the source. Sounds cannot travel in a vacuum. They can travel through solids, liquids, and gases. Sounds travel at different speeds through different media. Sounds travel faster in solids than liquids. Sounds travel slowest in gases. The loudness or softness of a sound is called intensity. The highness or lowness of a sound is called pitch. Sounds differ in intensity and pitch. Sounds can be reflected by objects and create an echo. Sounds can be sent over long distances. Percussion, wind, and stringed instruments make sounds in different ways.

CHECK YOURSELF

Write your answers on a sheet of paper.
1. A sound is made when an object
   a. does not move.
   c. is in a vacuum.
   b. vibrates.
   d. moves forward only.
2. The spreading out of air particles is called a
   a. compression.
   c. vacuum.
   b. rarefaction.
   d. pitch.
3. The crowding together of air particles is called a
   a. compression.
   c. media.
   b. rarefaction.
   d. sound.
4. What is a sound wave?
5. In what direction do sound waves travel from their source?
6. Name two stringed, two wind, and two percussion instruments.

7. Explain how each of the following instruments make sound: wind, stringed, percussion.
8. What is the word that means an empty space without air?
9. Name three media that sounds can travel through.
10. What is the speed of sound in air? water? wood?
11. In what medium do sounds travel the fastest?
12. What is meant by the pitch of a sound? the intensity of a sound?
13. List three things that affect the pitch of a vibrating string.
14. What is meant by the frequency of a sound? What is the frequency of sound we can hear?
15. To hear an echo, why must you stand at least 16.8 m (55 ft) from the reflecting object?
16. Explain how sounds are sent over long distances by telephone.

PROJECTS

1. Make a sound maker or a musical instrument. First look at or find pictures of instruments such as drums, clarinets, maracas, violins, and guitars. Select an instrument you would like to make. Then find materials around your home and classroom you could use to make the instrument. Play a tune on your instrument for your class.
2. Listen to some of your favorite singers or musicians. What instruments do you hear? Are the instruments winds (woodwinds or brass), stringed, or percussion? Do the singers have high or low pitched voices?
3. At the beginning of this unit you read about a tree falling in a forest with no one there. If a tree falls in a forest with no one there, is a sound made? Does a sound have to be heard to be a sound? Some scientists believe a sound is only made when someone is there to hear it. Other scientists think sounds do not depend on someone hearing them. Interview about ten people. Ask them these two questions. Report your findings to your class.

The people in the crowd hold their breath. In the air high above their heads, a young woman is about to risk her life. Suddenly she leaps from a trapeze, does a somersault, and reaches out for her partner's arms. The crowd roars as her partner catches her in mid air. Applause fills the tent.

These performers are excellent athletes. They are alert, their senses are sharp, and their bodies are in perfect condition.

You may never be a trapeze artist. But you can learn to keep your body in good physical condition. In this unit you will learn many things about your body. You will find out about some of your body parts and how they work.

UNIT 3
YOUR BODY: SENSING AND MOVING

 YOUR SENSES

1 SMELL

What would life be like if your nose were located on your elbow? your knee? the back of your head?

It is really nice to have your nose right where it is— beneath your eyes and above your mouth. You are able to smell how good (or bad) food is before you put it into your mouth. You can also smell the things you see. If it weren't for your nose, your glasses would fall down!

When you finish this lesson, you should be able to:

○ Tell the name given to the parts of your body that pick up information about what you smell, see, hear, taste, and touch.

○ Explain how your brain gets messages about smells.

Your nose is one of five **sense organs**. *Sense organs* are parts of your body that pick up information about the things you smell, see, hear, taste, and touch. To understand how your sense organs pick up information, you need to know something about **cells (sells)**.

Your body is made of tiny, tiny living parts called *cells*. Most of them are tinier than the period at the end of this sentence. Cells do different jobs depending on what kind of cells they are. **Nerve cells (nerve)** have the job of carrying information, or messages, from your sense organs to your brain. The picture shows a *nerve cell* as seen under a microscope.

Sense organs: Parts of your body that pick up information about the things you smell, see, hear, taste, and touch.

Cells: Tiny living parts your body is made of.

Nerve cells: Cells that carry information from your sense organs to your brain.

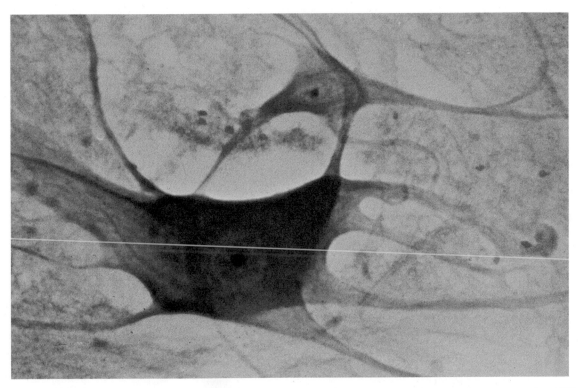

There are many nerve cells inside your nose. These cells are sensitive to odors. You probably have noticed that you can smell an odor even when the object with the odor is far away. How does the message about the odor get to your brain?

ACTIVITY

Materials
perfume or cologne
saucer

A. Remain in your seat but face the back of your classroom.

B. Your teacher will pour some perfume or cologne in a saucer.

C. Raise your hand as soon as you smell the odor.

D. When everyone in the class has smelled the odor, your teacher will tell you who smelled the odor first and who smelled it last.

During the activity, the perfume was at the front of the room. However, everyone in the room smelled the odor. The odor of the perfume was carried in all directions by the air in the room.

When you breathe in, air enters your nose through openings called **nostrils** (**noss**-trillz). On its way to your lungs, the air passes nerve cells in your nose. These nerve cells are branches of one main nerve called the **olfactory nerve** (ohl-**fack**-tore-ree). The *olfactory nerve* carries the smell message from your nose to your brain. The drawing on the next page will give you an idea of how smell messages get to your brain.

You smell air before it gets to your lungs. How might this be a safety device for your body?

Nostrils: The openings in your nose.

Olfactory nerve: The nerve that carries smell messages to your brain.

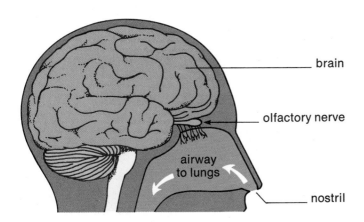

brain

olfactory nerve

airway
to lungs

nostril

MAIN IDEAS

Messages about smell are sent from your nose to your brain. Your nose is a sense organ. Nerve cells carry the messages. The nerve cells in your nose are sensitive to smell. Smell messages are carried to the brain by the olfactory nerve.

QUESTIONS

Write your answers on a sheet of paper.

1. What name is given to parts of your body that pick up information about what you smell, see, hear, taste and touch? Name the sense organ for smell.

2. While sitting in the living room, you smell dinner cooking in the kitchen. Explain how your brain gets the message about the smell.

2 SIGHT

Look carefully at this picture of people at a picnic. There are seven very strange things happening. Can you find them? When you finish this lesson, you should be able to:

○ Tell the names of and describe four parts of the eye.

○ Explain why the colored part of your eye changes in size.

○ Explain how your brain gets messages about sight.

When you studied the picture at the beginning of this lesson, your eyes were picking up information about what you saw. Your eyes are sense organs.

The colored part of the eye is called the **iris** (eye-russ). What color are your *irises?* In the center of each of your irises is an opening called the **pupil** (pew-pull). The *pupils* look like black dots. Light enters your eyes through the pupils.

Iris: The colored part of your eye.

Pupil: The opening in the center of your iris.

ACTIVITY

A. Look at your eye in the mirror. Draw a picture of the iris and pupil of your eye. Try to draw the picture the same size as your eye. Write the words *Normal Light* below your drawing.

B. Your teacher will dim the lights in your classroom. While the lights are dim, look at your eye. After 10 seconds draw another picture of your eye.

Write the words *Dim Light* below your drawing.

C. Your teacher will put the lights on. Look at your eye again for 10 seconds.

1. What happened to the size of your pupil when the light was dim?

2. What happened to the size of your pupil when the light was bright again?

Materials
mirror
paper
pencil

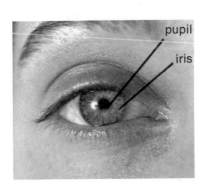

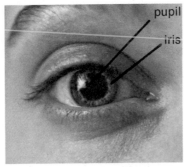

When the light was dim, your pupil appeared larger than when the light was bright. The pupils only appear to change size. It is really the iris that opens and closes. In dim light, the iris opens to let more light enter the eye. In bright light, the iris closes a little to stop too much light from entering. If too much light enters, parts of the eye can be damaged.

Lens: The part of your eye that changes light into a pattern.

After light enters your eye, it passes through a part of your eye called the **lens** (**lenz**). When the light passes through the *lens*, a pattern appears on the back of the eye. The pattern is an upside-down picture of the object you are looking at.

Optic nerve: The nerve that carries sight messages to your brain.

On the back of the inside of your eye are nerve cells. These nerve cells carry the message about the pattern to one main nerve. This nerve is called the **optic nerve** (**op**-tick). The *optic nerve* carries the sight message from the inside of your eye, or sense organ, to your brain. Your brain changes the upside-down pattern so that you see the object right side up.

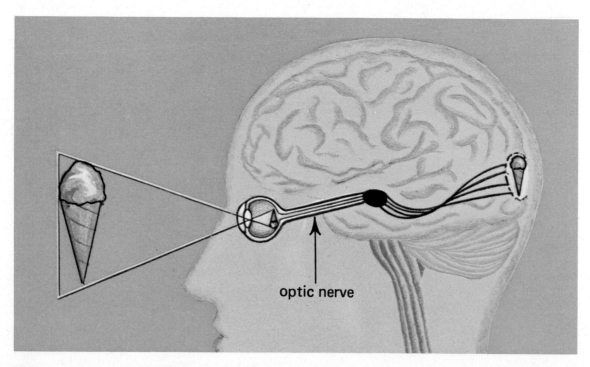

optic nerve

The eye is a sense organ. Parts of the eye are the iris, pupil, lens, and optic nerve. The iris can change in size. Sight messages are carried to the brain by the optic nerve.

QUESTIONS

Write your answers on a sheet of paper.

1. Tell the names of four parts of your eye and describe each part.
2. If you were in a dark room, what would happen to your irises? Why? What would happen if you went outdoors into the bright sunlight?
3. Explain how your brain gets sight messages.

SOMETHING EXTRA

Do you think your nose is sensitive? Can you sometimes smell odors that your friends cannot smell?

A bloodhound has a very sensitive nose. This dog can smell odors that human beings do not even know are there!

Bloodhounds can be trained to follow an odor, or scent, over long distances and through thick forests. These special dogs have been very helpful in finding lost people and escaped criminals.

First the bloodhound smells an article of clothing the person has worn. Then it sniffs the ground where the person was last seen. The dog's very sensitive nose usually is able to follow the scent right to the person.

3 HEARING

What sounds would you hear if you were at the motor-cycle race in the picture? You probably would hear the sounds of the motors and the screech of the tires. You might also hear the cheers of the crowd.

Some sounds are loud like the sounds at a motorcycle race. Others are soft like the sound of rain falling on the ground. How do you know when you have heard a sound? When you finish this lesson, you should be able to:

○ Tell the name of and describe parts of your ear.

○ Explain how your brain gets messages about what you hear.

A sound is made when something **vibrates** (vi-brayts). When something *vibrates* it moves back and forth. A vibrating object makes the air around it vibrate. The air carries the sound vibrations in all directions. How do sound vibrations in the air become sounds you hear?

The sound vibration is picked up by one of your sense organs. What do you think is your sense organ for hearing?

The ear you see when you look in a mirror is not your whole ear. It is the part of your ear called the **outer ear**. Your *outer ears* gather sound vibrations. Your outer ears work like funnels. They direct the sound vibrations into another part of your ear called the **ear canal**. Your *ear canal* is a narrow tube that begins at the inner side of the outer ear. The ear canal carries the sound vibrations into your head.

Vibrate: To move back and forth.

Outer ear: The part of your ear that gathers sound vibrations.

Ear canal: A narrow tube inside your ear that carries sound vibrations into your head.

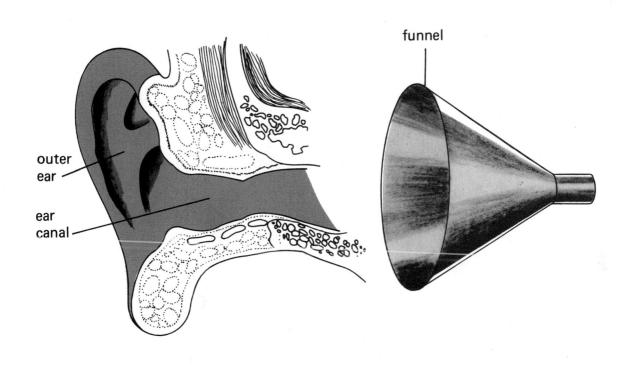

funnel

outer ear

ear canal

Eardrum: The part of your ear at the end of the ear canal.

At the end of your ear canal is the **eardrum**. The sound vibrations that have traveled through the ear canal then strike the *eardrum*. The eardrum also starts to vibrate. The vibrations from your eardrum pass along to nearby bones. These bones are very tiny. They begin to vibrate too.

Around the small bones are nerve cells. The nerve cells carry the message about the vibrations to one main nerve. This nerve is called the **auditory nerve** (awe-dih-tore-ree). The *auditory nerve* carries the sound message to your brain. When your brain receives the message, you know you have heard a sound.

Auditory nerve: The nerve that carries sound messages to your brain.

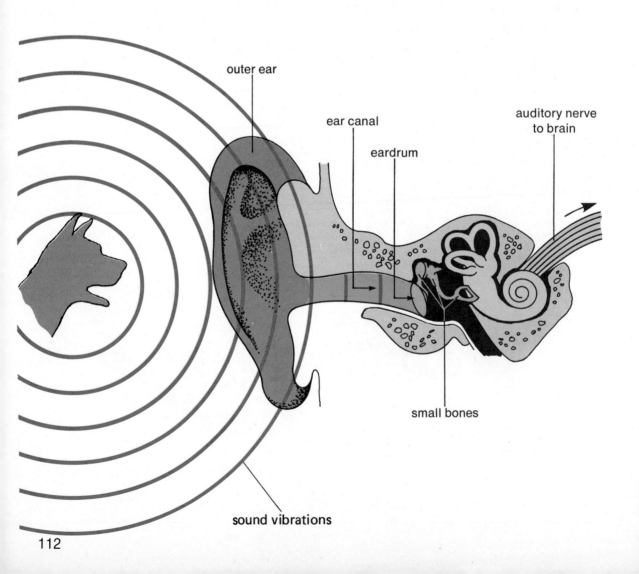

outer ear

ear canal

eardrum

auditory nerve to brain

small bones

sound vibrations

A sound is made when an object vibrates. The sound vibrations travel through the air to your ear. Parts of your ear gather and direct the sounds into your head. The sound vibrations are passed along through your ear to the auditory nerve. The auditory nerve sends the sound message to your brain.

QUESTIONS

Write your answers on a sheet of paper.
Wendy is roller-skating outside. She hears her mother call, "Wendy, come in for dinner."

1. What part of Wendy's ear gathered the sound vibrations?
2. What part of Wendy's ear is between the outer ear and eardrum?
3. What happened to Wendy's eardrum when the sound vibrations struck it?
4. How did the sound message get from her eardrum to her brain?

4 TASTE

Look at the above picture for a few seconds. How would the lemon taste if you touched it to your tongue? Would the expression on your face tell the answer?

The lemon probably would taste sour. Tasting or thinking of sour things can make your lips pucker. Did you know that if you eat a lemon in front of trumpet players they will probably stop playing? Watching you may make their lips pucker, and they will be unable to blow through the horns.

When you finish this lesson, you should be able to:

○ Tell the names given to two parts of your tongue.

○ Explain how your brain gets messages about tastes.

○ List the four types of tastes.

Most people recognize four kinds of tastes: sweet, sour, salty, and bitter. Can you group the foods in the picture according to these tastes?

Taste buds: Groups of cells on your tongue.

Taste nerves: Nerves that carry taste messages to your brain.

What part of your body do you think is the sense organ for taste? If you think it is your tongue, you are right! On your tongue are groups of cells called **taste buds**. *Taste buds* contain **taste nerves**. *Taste nerves* send taste messages from the sense organ to your brain. Your brain tells you if the taste is sweet, sour, salty, or bitter.

Some foods are combinations of two or more tastes. For example, barbecue sauce has a taste that is hard to classify. It is both sweet and sour.

Here is an activity in which you will taste and group foods as sweet, sour, salty, or bitter. You will need a partner.

ACTIVITY

Materials
blindfold
5 food samples in numbered paper cups
paper
2 paper cups with water
pencil
10 toothpicks

A. Your teacher will give you five food samples, each in a numbered paper cup.

B. Decide who will be the taster. Blindfold the taster. The taster should hold the nostrils closed.

C. With the flat end of the toothpick, pick up a small amount of one food sample. Place the food sample on the taster's tongue.

D. Tell the taster to spread the sample around with the tongue. Then ask the taster to identify the type of taste and name the food. Write the number of the sample and the taster's answer on your paper.

E. Repeat steps C and D with each sample. Have the taster drink some water after each sample. Use a new toothpick each time.

F. Now switch places and repeat the activity.

You probably were able to group most of the samples as either sweet, sour, salty, or bitter. Different groups of taste buds on your tongue react to the different types of tastes. The taste buds for each type of taste are located in different areas on your tongue. Here is a drawing that shows approximately where the taste buds of each type are located.

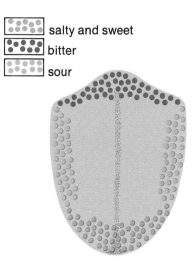

salty and sweet

bitter

sour

Besides giving you information about the taste of a food, your sense of taste is helpful in another way. How do you know if a food is unsafe to eat? Can you think of any time when your sense of taste helped you to know that a food was unsafe?

MAIN IDEAS

Your tongue is a sense organ. Taste buds and taste nerves pick up and send taste messages to your brain. There are four types of tastes.

QUESTIONS

Write your answers on a sheet of paper.

1. What are the names given to the two parts of your tongue that pick up and send taste messages?

2. When you eat a food, you know immediately how it tastes. Explain how your brain gets the taste message.

3. What are the four types of tastes?

5 TOUCH

Has anyone ever told you never to touch a hot iron? The boy in the picture above wasn't so lucky! Besides heat, what else do you think he is feeling? How do you know when you feel heat or pain?

When you finish this lesson, you should be able to:

○ List five kinds of messages your skin can pick up.

○ Tell the name given to nerve cells in your skin.

○ Explain how your brain gets messages from the skin.

Your skin is a sense organ. It is the largest sense organ you have. Your skin can pick up messages about heat, cold, pain, touch, and pressure. In your skin are many nerve cells. These nerve cells are called **receptors** (ree-**sep**-tores). Each *receptor* senses only one kind of message. Your skin has receptors for heat, cold, pain, touch, and pressure.

Receptors: The nerve cells in your skin.

Look at the girl in the picture. What messages is her skin picking up about the rabbit? The receptors in her skin are picking up messages about touch, pressure, and perhaps heat from the rabbit's body.

Receptors are not evenly spread out over your skin. Some places have more receptors than others. Your skin is more sensitive in the places that have more receptors and would pick up more messages there. Your skin is less sensitive in places that have fewer receptors and would not pick up as many messages there. Some receptors are deeper within your skin than others.

Materials
paper clip
ruler

A. Get a partner. Decide who will be tested first.

B. Unbend the paper clip and reshape it as shown in the picture. The ends of the clip should be about 1 cm ($\frac{1}{2}$ in.) apart.

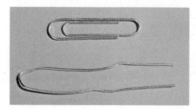

C. The person being tested should roll up a sleeve. Eyes should be closed.

D. Gently touch the end of the clip to the person's finger as shown in the pictures. Do this a total of four times. Ask the person to say whether one or two ends were felt.

E. Repeat step D on the palm, back of hand, and arm.

F. Switch places and repeat the activity.

1. At which places were you and your partner best able to feel the correct number of paper clip ends?

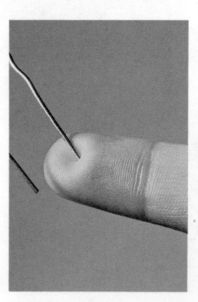

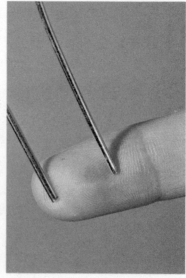

Your fingertips are more sensitive than the back of your hand. There are more touch receptors there. Touch receptors lie close to the skin's surface. Pressure receptors lie deep within the skin. If the paper clip end is moved over your skin lightly, you feel only touch. If the clip is pressed against your skin, you feel touch and pressure. What would you feel if the clip was pressed too hard against your skin?

The receptors are the starting point for messages that go to your brain. Other nerves take the message from the receptors to the **spinal cord** (**spy**-nahl **cord**). The *spinal cord* is a large nerve that carries the messages about heat, cold, pain, touch, and pressure to your brain.

Spinal cord: A large nerve that carries messages to your brain.

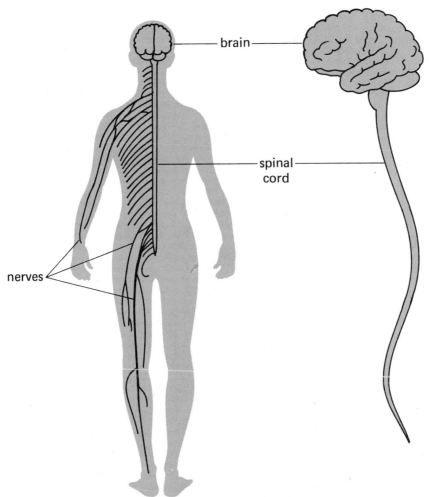

brain

spinal cord

nerves

Nervous system: Your sense organs, nerves, brain, and spinal cord.

Your sense organs, nerves, brain, and spinal cord make up your **nervous system**. A system is a group of body parts that work together to perform a job. Your *nervous system's* job is to gather, send, and understand the things around you.

MAIN IDEAS

Your skin is a sense organ. Near the surface of your skin are special nerve cells that gather information. They are called receptors. There are receptors for heat, cold, pain, pressure, and touch. Some parts of your skin are more sensitive than others because they have more receptors. Receptors in your skin carry the information, or the messages, to other nerves and then to the spinal cord. The messages are carried to your brain.

QUESTIONS

Write your answers on a sheet of paper.

1. List five kinds of messages your skin can pick up.

2. What is the name given to nerve cells in your skin?

3. Imagine you have fallen and scraped your knee. How does the message get from the sense organ to your brain? Would all the different kinds of receptors be affected?

CHAPTER 8

BONES, MUSCLES, AND HEALTH

1 BONES

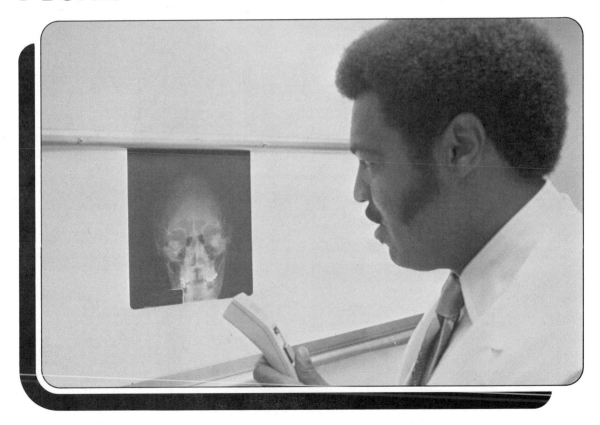

Have you ever broken any of your bones? The doctor in this picture is checking an X ray to be sure that the patient did not break a bone. If the doctor finds a break, the patient will need medical treatment.

When you finish this lesson, you should be able to:

○ Tell three reasons why your bones are important.

○ Tell the names of and describe where four bones in your body are located.

○ Tell the name given to a soft substance in some bones.

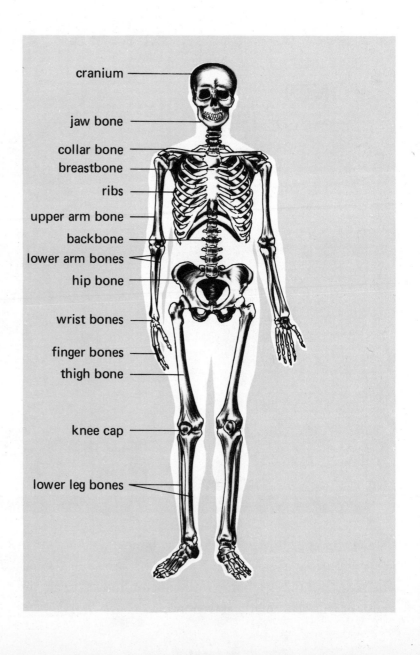

cranium

jaw bone

collar bone

breastbone

ribs

upper arm bone

backbone

lower arm bones

hip bone

wrist bones

finger bones

thigh bone

knee cap

lower leg bones

The bones in your body are like a frame that gives you support. Some of the bones help you move. All the bones in your body make up your **skeletal system (skel-eh-tal)**.

There are 206 bones in your *skeletal system*. The bones are different shapes and sizes. There are round ones, flat ones, long ones, and short ones. Every bone has a special job. Many bones protect important parts of your body. To study the skeletal system let us start with the bones in your head and end with the bones in your feet. As you read about each bone, refer back to the drawing on page 124 to find the bone.

The doctor in the picture on page 123 is looking at an X ray of the bones in the patient's head. The group of bones that surround the brain make up the **cranium (kray-nee-um)**.

The *cranium* protects the brain. The cranium is strong but it can be cracked if the person receives a severe hit on the head. People that play certain sports or work in certain jobs wear protection for their cranium. Look at the people in the pictures. What are they doing? How do they protect their craniums from injury?

Skeletal system: All the bones in your body.

Cranium: The group of bones that surround the brain.

Jawbone: A bone that is part of your head.

Backbone: A bone that is found in the center of your back.

Vertebrae: The small bones that make up the backbone.

Another bone that is part of your head is your **jawbone**. Touch your chin and move your hand up toward your ear. The bone you feel is your *jawbone*. The movement of the jawbone allows you to chew food and speak.

The bone shown in the first drawing below is a large bone that goes up the center of your back. It is called your **backbone**. One end of your *backbone* is connected to your head; the other end is connected to your hip bones.

Your backbone is actually made of many small bones. Gently rub your backbone with one hand. Can you feel some of the small bones? They are called **vertebrae** (ver-tih-bray). Your backbone has twenty-four *vertebrae*.

Look at the drawing of one vertebra. Each vertebra has an opening through its center. Your spinal cord passes through these openings. The spinal cord is protected by the vertebrae of the backbone.

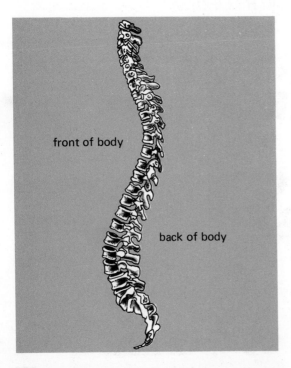

front of body

back of body

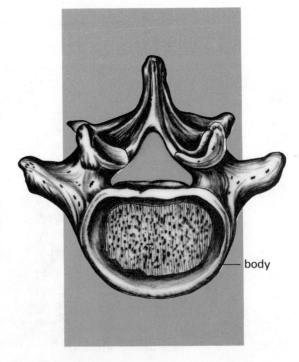

body

Connected to your backbone are twelve pairs of bones called **ribs**. The *ribs* come around to the front of your body. At the front of your body, the upper seven pairs are connected to a bone called the breastbone. The ribs form a cage that protects the heart and lungs.

Attached to the bottom of your backbone are two large hip bones. These hip bones and your backbone form the **pelvis** (**pell**-vis). The *pelvis* bones bear the weight of the body.

The upper part of each leg and each arm has one large bone. The lower parts of your legs and arms have two bones. Your hands and feet have many small bones. Your hands have more bones than any other part of your body. Look at the X ray of a hand. How many bones can you count?

Many bones are hollow inside. The hollow space is filled with a soft substance called **marrow** (**mar**-row). There are two types of *marrow*. Red marrow is found in flat bones, such as ribs. Yellow marrow is found in long bones, such as leg bones.

Ribs: Twelve pairs of bones.

Pelvis: The hip bones and backbone.

Marrow: A soft substance in the hollow of some bones.

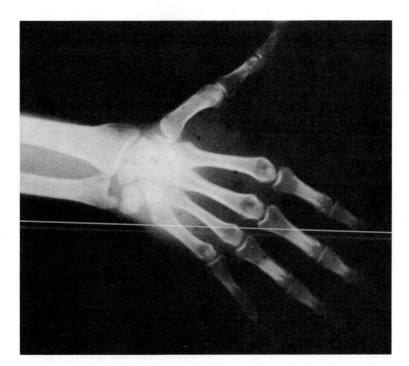

The bones in your body make up your skeletal system. Your bones give your body support, help you move, and protect some body parts. There are 206 bones in your body. Some bones have a soft material in them called marrow.

QUESTIONS

Write your answers on a sheet of paper.

1. What are three ways in which your bones are important?
2. Tell the names of four bones in your body. Where is each bone located? Why is each bone important?
3. What is the soft substance in the hollow space in some bones? List two types.

SOMETHING EXTRA

Bones can break or chip. Muscles can be strained or torn. When these injuries occur, it is necessary to get medical treatment. Most physicians know how to treat bone and muscle injuries.

Sometimes, people with muscle or bone diseases or injuries cannot move or do things as they once did. They need help in learning how to adjust to their problem. **Physical therapists** (**fizz**-eh-kal **ther**-ah-pists) are people who help people with such diseases or injuries. *Physical therapists* help their patients exercise and teach them how to carry out everyday activities. Most physical therapists work in hospitals or nursing homes.

2 WHERE BONES MEET

Look at the picture above. How do you think the baby's skeletal system is different from the adult's?

You probably said the baby's bones are smaller. They are also softer. When you were a newborn baby, some of your bones were made of a soft substance. As you grew older, your bones became harder.

When you finish this lesson, you should be able to:

○ Tell the name given to the soft substance between some bones.

○ Name and describe the places where two bones meet.

○ Explain what holds bones in place at the point where they meet.

Cartilage: A soft substance that is found where some bones meet.

Joint: The place where two bones meet.

Hinge joint: A kind of joint.

Ball-and-socket joint: A kind of joint.

Babies' bones are made of a soft substance called **cartilage** (kar-till-lij). Most of your bones are hard. However, you do have *cartilage* at the end of your nose and in places where some bones meet. The place where two bones meet is called a **joint**. At some *joints*, the bones are able to move. The cartilage at the joint is like a padding that keeps the ends of the bones from rubbing together when they move.

You have three kinds of moveable joints. One kind is like the hinge on a door. It is called a **hinge joint.** The bones at a *hinge joint* can move back and forth or up and down. The joints in your elbows and knees are hinge joints. So are the joints in your fingers and toes.

Another kind of moveable joint is the **ball-and-socket joint.** At a *ball-and-socket joint,* the end of one bone is shaped like a ball. It fits into a curved space at the end of the other bone. Bones at this kind of joint can move in many directions. The joints in your shoulders and hips are ball-and-socket joints.

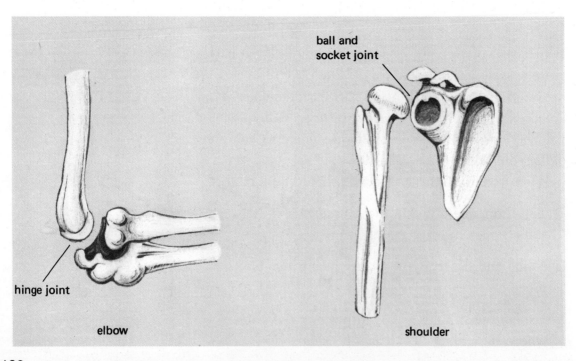

ball and socket joint

hinge joint

elbow

shoulder

A third kind of joint is the **pivot joint**. The bones at a *pivot joint* can move around and back. The joint where your head meets your backbone is a pivot joint.

Pivot joint: A kind of joint.

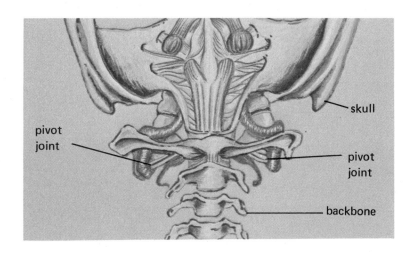

What keeps bones from sliding off each other when they move? Bones at these three types of joints are held together by strong bands of material called **ligaments** (lig-ah-ments). *Ligaments* stretch across joints from the end of one bone to the end of the other. Ligaments hold the bones in place. Look at the drawing. Can you find the joint, bones, and ligaments?

Ligaments: Strong bands of material that hold bones in place at joints.

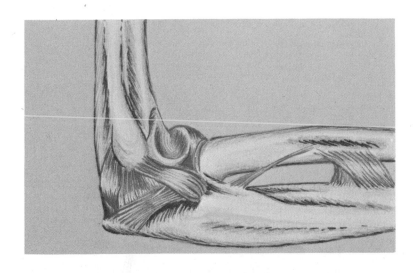

When you are born, some of your bones are made of cartilage. As you grow up, your bones become hard. You have cartilage at some joints. There are three kinds of joints: hinge, ball and socket, and pivot.

QUESTIONS

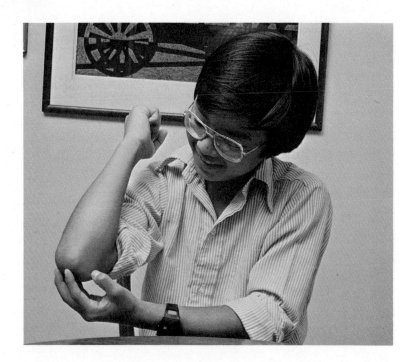

Write your answers on a sheet of paper.

1. What is the soft substance between some bones that keeps them from rubbing together?
2. Name three kinds of joints. Which joint is found in the place the boy is holding? How are joints different from each other?
3. What holds bones in place at a joint?

3 MUSCLES

As you read this book, your eyes are moving. You are able to make your eyes move from left to right as you read each sentence. You are also able to stop the movement if you wish. Can you think of a movement of a part of your eye that you cannot control as well?

When you finish this lesson, you should be able to:

○ Tell the words that describe muscles you can and cannot control.

○ Name two muscles in your arm.

○ Explain what happens when a muscle contracts.

As you read your eyelids move. They move down over your eyes and then back up again. You are able to blink when you want. However, you cannot stop yourself from blinking forever. Blinking is a movement you cannot completely control.

Every movement you make is caused by muscles. Some muscles you can control. They are called **voluntary muscles** (**vohl**-un-teh-ree). Your arm and leg muscles are *voluntary muscles*. You can move your arm and leg muscles when you want to. Look at the drawing below. It shows the muscles in the upper part of your arm. The muscle on the top side of your arm is called the **bicep** (**by**-sep). The muscle on the underside of your arm is called the **tricep** (**try**-sep). The *bicep* and *tricep* work together to move your arm. They are voluntary muscles.

Look at the drawing again. What are the muscles attached to? Most voluntary muscles are attached to bones.

Voluntary muscles: Muscles you can control.

Bicep: The muscle on the top side of your upper arm.

Tricep: The muscle on the bottom side of your upper arm.

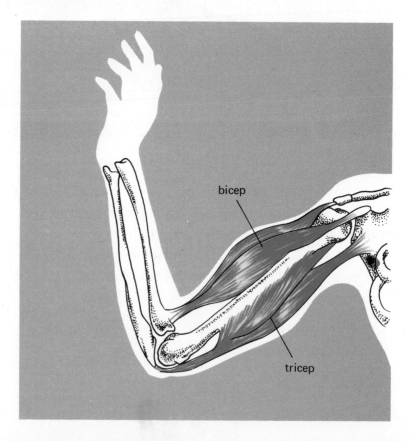

bicep

tricep

Some muscles are attached directly to the bones. Others are attached to the bones by **tendons** (ten-dahns). Can you find the *tendons* in the drawing on page 134?

Tendons: Attach muscles to bones.

Materials
3 books

A. Find a partner.

B. Roll up the sleeve on your right arm.

C. Put your arm on your desk top with your elbow resting on the surface.

D. Have your partner place three books in your open hand.

E. With the books in your hand, raise your arm. At the same time, look at the part of your arm where your bicep is found.

1. What happened to your bicep as you lifted your arm?

When you want to move your arm, your brain sends a message to the muscle. The muscle shortens and becomes firm as the movement occurs. We say the muscle contracts. When you want to stop the movement, your brain tells the muscle to relax. Did you see your bicep shorten? How do you think it would have felt if you touched it?

Look at the drawing below. It shows some of your muscles. Can you find the biceps and triceps?

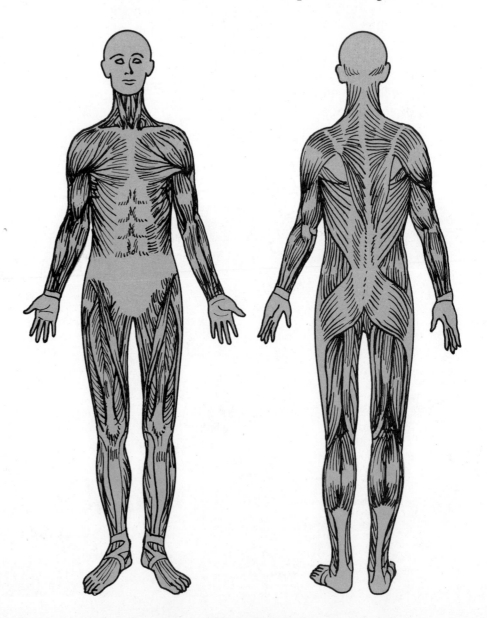

Some muscles you cannot control. They are called **involuntary muscles** (in-**vohl**-un-teh-ree). Your heart is an *involuntary muscle*. You cannot control this muscle. It contracts and relaxes on its own. The muscles in your stomach contract and relax whether you want them to or not. They are involuntary muscles too. The muscles that move your eyelids are both voluntary and unvoluntary. So are the muscles that help you breathe. You cannot totally control them. Involuntary muscles, unlike voluntary muscles, are not attached to bones.

Involuntary muscles: Muscles you cannot control.

MAIN IDEAS

Every movement you make is caused by muscles. Some muscles you can control; others you cannot. Some muscles are attached directly to bones. Others are attached to bones by tendons. Muscles contract and relax.

QUESTIONS

Write your answers on a sheet of paper.

1. What word describes a muscle you can control? a muscle you cannot control?
2. Name two muscles in your arm.
3. What happens when a muscle contracts?

4 MORE ABOUT MUSCLES

Which person in the picture do you think is stronger? You probably said the one with the bulging muscles. However, bulging muscles are not always the strongest muscles.

When you finish this lesson, you should be able to:

○ Tell the name of the system that includes all the muscles in your body.

○ Name and describe three types of muscles.

Muscular system: All the muscles in your body.

All the muscles in your body make up your **muscular system**. There are about 400 muscles in your *muscular system*. In the last lesson you learned the names of two of them. Can you name those muscles? Where on your body are they found?

Every muscle in your body contains thousands of tiny muscle cells. There are three types of muscles in your body. The muscle cells look different.

One type of muscle is called **smooth muscle**. The cells of *smooth muscles* are long, thin, and pointed at each end. Look at the first drawing below. It shows a group of smooth muscle cells. Do you see a dark area in the center of each cell? This area is called the **nucleus** (new-klee-us). Almost all the cells in your body have *nuclei*. Each smooth muscle cell has one nucleus in its center. The muscles in your stomach are smooth muscles.

Another type of muscle in your body is **cardiac** (kar-dee-ak) **muscle**. The word *cardiac* means of or near the heart. Your heart is made of *cardiac muscle*. Look at the second drawing. The cells of cardiac muscles look striped. They have dark and light bands across them. The cells of cardiac muscle branch out and weave together. Each cell has one nucleus.

Smooth muscle: A type of muscle.

Nucleus: Part of a cell.

Cardiac muscle: A type of muscle.

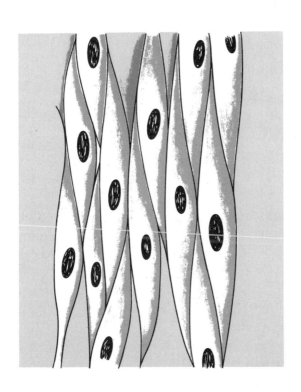

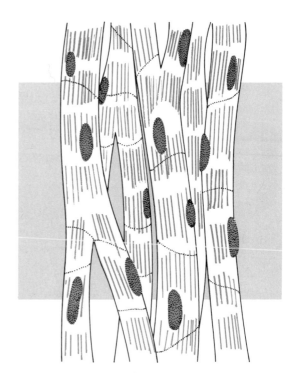

Skeletal muscle: A type of muscle.

The third type of muscle is called **skeletal muscle**. The cells of *skeletal muscles* are long and cylinder-shaped like straws. Look at the drawing. These cells have dark and light bands across them. What other type of muscle has dark and light bands? Your tongue and lips are skeletal muscles. So are your biceps and triceps.

Some skeletal muscles are attached to bones by tendons. When the muscle contracts, the tendons and bones move too.

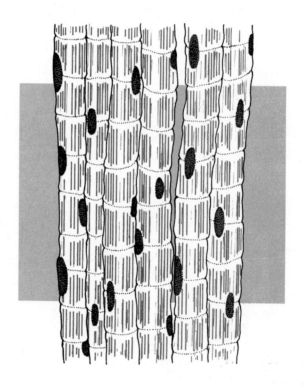

Materials
none

A. Hold your hands out, palms down, in front of you.

B. Move your fingers as if you were playing a piano. At the same time, look at the backs of your hands.

1. What do you see on the backs of your hands as your fingers moved?

C. Continue the movement for two minutes.

2. How do your arms feel?

You were able to see your tendons moving when you looked at your hands. The tendons were moved by the muscles in your arm. The muscles in your arm moved your finger bones. After awhile, your arm muscle felt tired.

Smooth and cardiac muscles are involuntary. Your heart muscles contract and relax on their own. So do your stomach muscles. Skeletal muscles are voluntary. Your biceps and triceps, for example, move when you want them to.

MAIN IDEAS

All the muscles in your body make up your muscular system. You have about 400 muscles. There are three types of muscles in your body.

QUESTIONS

Write your answers on a sheet of paper.

1. What system is made of the 400 muscles in your body?

2. Name three types of muscles.

3. How are the three types of muscles different? Name a part of the body as an example of where each type is found.

5 YOUR HEALTH

The runners are at the starting line. They listen carefully for the signal. "On your mark! Get set! Go!" The runners are off. Their legs move rapidly over the ground. Their arms stretch to balance their bodies. Their eyes are fixed on the finish line.

These runners are excellent athletes. Their body systems are working properly. Which body systems are being used?

When you finish this lesson, you should be able to:

○ List three things your body systems need to work properly.

○ Explain how alcohol, drugs, and tobacco can be harmful to your body systems.

The runners in the picture on page 142 are using their nervous, skeletal, and muscular systems. Their sense organs are gathering sound and sight messages. The voluntary muscles in their arms and legs are contracting and relaxing. Their muscles are moving their bones. If their body systems were not working properly, how would their running be affected? What do you think might cause body systems to work improperly? How can you keep your body systems in good shape?

Good eating habits are important for all your body systems. Eating a great deal of food does not mean the body systems will work well. You must eat the right kinds of foods. For example, milk is very good for the growth of strong bones. Children with a low-milk diet may develop soft, crooked bones. Egg yolks, fresh vegetables, and cod liver oil are also good for your bones.

The muscles in your body need to be exercised. If they are not, they become weak and flabby. When you exercise you should first "warm up," or do easy exercises. This will prevent muscle injuries such as muscle strains or tears.

Your muscles also need rest. So do all your body systems. You should always try to get a good night's sleep. Without rest, the runners at the race would not be able to run their best.

The right kinds of food, exercise, and rest will help your body systems work properly.

Alcohol is a beverage that can be harmful to the body systems. When people drink alcohol, their nervous and muscular systems do not work well because alcohol affects the brain. The brain is then unable to control the muscles. People who drink too much alcohol cannot walk properly. They often stumble and fall.

The sense organs are also affected by alcohol. Sight is often blurred or doubled. People who drink too much alcohol often speak loudly. This is because they cannot hear as well as usual.

Drugs can be grouped in two ways: prescription drugs and over-the-counter drugs. Prescription drugs are used for medical reasons. They are helpful in fighting illness or infection. You are told to take them by a doctor. You are given directions about their use. Over-the-counter drugs are those you find on the shelves in a drugstore. The package usually gives directions about their use.

Some drugs are addictive. This means that the person's body needs an ongoing supply of the drug when there is no medical need for the drug. **Cocaine** (ko-**kane**), **morphine** (**mor**-feen), and **heroin** (hehr-oh-in) can be addictive drugs. Some people use these drugs because they think the drugs make them feel good. However, these drugs are not good for their body systems. The use of *cocaine* and *heroin* is against the law.

Cocaine: A drug. Morphine and heroin: Addictive drugs.

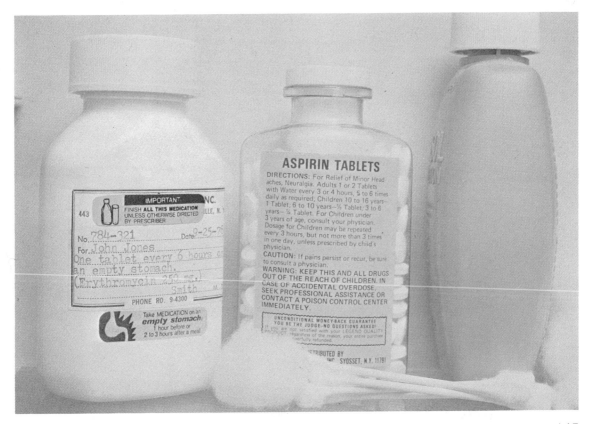

Any drug is dangerous if not used properly. For example, over 100 children die each year from misusing aspirin. Many drugs affect the nervous and muscular systems in the same ways as alcohol. Some drugs cause the pupil in the eye to widen. This is dangerous if the person is in bright light. Too much light enters the eye, and the inside of the eye can be damaged.

Tobacco is a plant. Cigarettes and cigars are made with tobacco. Tobacco contains two poisonous substances: **nicotine** (**nik**-koe-teen) and **tar.** *Nicotine* and cigarette or cigar smoke can cause a shortness of breath in a smoker. This means that a smoker could have difficulty breathing when exercising. Tobacco affects the muscles you use to breathe. *Tar* can cause disease, such as cancer, in humans.

Marijuana (mar-eh-**wah**-nah) is a plant. It can be used as a drug. The leaves of the plant are dried, cut into tiny pieces, and made into short cigarettes. When smoked, *marijuana* has a similar effect on the nervous and muscular systems as alcohol. The pictures on the next page show a marijuana plant and cigarette. In some states using or selling marijuana is against the law.

Nicotine: A poisonous substance in tobacco.

Tar: A poisonous substance in tobacco.

Marijuana: A plant that can be used as a drug.

146

MAIN
IDEAS

The right kinds of food, exercise, and rest will help your body systems work properly. Alcohol, drugs, and tobacco can be harmful to your body systems.

QUESTIONS

Write your answers on a sheet of paper.

1. List three things your body systems need to work properly.
2. How does alcohol affect your nervous system?
3. How can the use of drugs cause eye damage?
4. What are two harmful effects of nicotine and tar?

The nervous system gives you information about the things you smell, see, hear, taste, and touch. It is made up of the sense organs, nerves, brain, and spinal cord.

The skeletal system gives you support, helps you move, and protects important body parts. There are 206 bones in your skeletal system. The place where two bones meet is called a joint. Three types of joints are hinge, ball and socket, and pivot.

Every movement you make is caused by your muscular system. There are about 400 muscles in your body. Muscles are either voluntary or involuntary.

The right kinds of food, exercise, and rest will help your body systems work properly. Alcohol, tobacco, and drugs can be harmful to your body systems.

CHECK YOURSELF

1. Match each nerve with its sense.
   a. receptors   sight
   b. olfactory nerve   hearing
   c. optic nerve   taste
   d. taste nerves   smell
   e. auditory nerve   touch
2. Name five sense organs.
3. What name is given to the small openings through which air enters your nose?
4. How does bright light affect the iris and pupil of the eye?
5. Where is your outer ear? your ear canal? your eardrum?
6. What are the four types of tastes?
7. Name five types of skin receptors.

8. What system is made up of your sense organs, nerves, brain, and spinal cord?
9. Name five bones in your body and tell where each is located.
10. What is a joint? Name three types of joints and give an example of each.
11. How are voluntary and involuntary muscles different from each other?
12. What happens to your bicep as movement occurs?
13. What are the three types of muscles in your body? Give an example of each.
14. Why are the right kinds of food, exercise, and rest important?
15. Name three things that can be harmful to your body systems.

PROJECTS

1. Put small amounts of food samples in paper cups. Blindfold a classmate. Give the classmate a cup with a food sample and ask the classmate to smell the contents. While the classmate is sniffing, write the name of the sample on the chalkboard so the rest of the class can see it. Ask the classmate to name the food sample sniffed. If the classmate is right, the class should say the word *SENSE*. If the classmate is wrong, the class should say *NONSENSE*. Repeat the activity with different classmates each sniffing a different sample.
2. Find out how a camera is like the human eye. What part of a camera is like the iris, pupil, lens, and back of the eye? How does a photographer control the light entering the camera? Is the light pattern upside down on the film in the camera? Write a report about your findings. Present your report to your class.

The robots in the picture can do some of the things you can do. They can walk, move their arms and heads, make sounds, and maybe even speak. Robots have been shown in books and movies as heroes, villains, companions, and helpers, just as humans have. However, have you ever seen a wounded robot bleed? Does a robot eat or breathe? Humans do!

In this unit you will find out about the systems in your body involved in eating, breathing, and moving blood around your body.

4 YOUR BODY: STAYING ALIVE

CHAPTER

FOOD AND HEALTH

1 WHY IS FOOD IMPORTANT?

What did you eat for breakfast this morning? Have you eaten lunch? How do you think you would feel if you hadn't eaten breakfast or lunch?

When you finish this lesson, you should be able to:

○ Name six important chemicals found in food.

○ Explain the importance of some of these chemicals.

○ Tell how to test a food for starch.

If you did not eat today, you probably feel hungry and tired. You feel tired because your body is not getting the **energy** (en-err-jee) it needs. *Energy* is needed to do work. Work can be running in a race, reading a book, or cleaning your room.

Energy: The ability to do work.

Your body must grow and repair itself. For example, if you break a bone in your arm, your body must repair the broken bone. In order to repair itself, your body must take in food. How does food supply energy and aid in the growth and repair of the body?

Food contains **nutrients** (new-tree-ents). *Nutrients* are chemicals that your body needs for growth, repair, and energy. Below is a chart that lists the nutrients found in food. Are any of the nutrients' names familiar to you? The chart also includes examples of food sources for each nutrient.

Nutrients: Chemicals that your body needs for growth, repair, and energy.

nutrients	food sources
carbohydrates	
starch	bread, spaghetti, rice
sugar	honey, candy, pastry
fats	butter, oils, nuts
protein	lean meat, fish, eggs, cheese, milk, peas, nuts
minerals	milk, leafy vegetables, liver, seafood, raisins
vitamins	vegetables, milk, eggs, citrus fruits, whole grain cereals
water	all foods

Carbohydrates: The nutrients sugar and starch.

Iodine: A chemical used to test a food for starch.

Carbohydrates (kar-bow-**hi**-drates) and fats are the nutrients that supply energy. *Carbohydrates* are often divided into two groups: sugars and starches. A food can be tested to find out if it contains starch. In the test a chemical called **iodine** (**eye**-oh-dine) is used. *Iodine* is a dark red liquid.

Materials
iodine
medicine dropper
paper towel
peeled piece of potato
several grains of
  cooked rice
1 slice of bread
1 slice of cucumber
1 slice of an orange

A. Place the food items on the paper towel.

B. Using the medicine dropper, place 3 drops of iodine on the slice of bread.

  1. What happened to the color of iodine?

C. Repeat step B with each food item.

  2. What happened to the color of the iodine when you dropped it on each food item?

Iodine is a chemical used to test a food for starch. If the food contains starch, the iodine changes color. The iodine changes from a dark red color to black. Bread, potatoes, and rice are foods that contain starch. What foods tested in the activity did not contain starch? Although starches and sugars (carbohydrates) supply energy, you may eat more of them than your body needs. When this happens, the extra carbohydrates change into body fat.

The nutrient needed by the body to grow and repair itself is **protein** (**pro**-teen). Look back at the chart of nutrients on page 153. What foods contain *protein*? What foods contain minerals and vitamins?

Protein: A nutrient needed for growth and repair of the body.

MAIN IDEAS

Food contains chemicals that your body needs for growth, repair, and energy. These chemicals are called nutrients. Carbohydrates and fats supply energy. Protein is important for the growth and repair of the body. A food can be tested for starch.

QUESTIONS

Write your answers on a sheet of paper.

1. What are nutrients? Name six nutrients.
2. Why are carbohydrates important?
3. Why is protein important?
4. How can you find out if cooked spaghetti contains starch?

2 WHAT TO EAT

In many schools, a school lunch is served. Have you ever eaten a school lunch? Do you know who plans the school lunch menu?

When you finish this lesson, you should be able to:

○ Tell the word that describes a diet that includes the right amounts of all the nutrients.

○ List the four food groups.

○ Name the units used to measure the amount of energy a food will supply.

The school **dietician** (die-et-**tish**-shun) plans the school lunch menu. When planning the menu, the *dietician* must be aware of the nutrients each food contains. The foods chosen for the meal must contain all the nutrients. A diet that includes the right amounts of all the nutrients the body needs is called a **balanced diet**. A *balanced diet* is important for good health. How can you be sure you have a balanced diet?

Foods are divided into four groups: the milk group, the bread-cereal group, the meat group, and the vegetable-fruit group. Look at the chart below. It lists some of the foods contained in each food group. What foods are in the milk group? bread-cereal group? meat group? vegetable-fruit group?

Dietician: A person who plans meals that contain all the nutrients.

Balanced diet: A diet that includes the right amounts of all the nutrients the body needs.

milk group	bread–cereal group	meat group	vegetable–fruit group
milk	bread	meat	green vegetables
cheese	noodles	chicken	yellow vegetables
butter	rice	fish	oranges
ice cream	spaghetti	eggs	grapefruits
	pancakes	nuts	tomatoes
	whole grain cereals	peas	

The chart below shows the amount of food items from each group that you should have each day.

food group	amounts you should have each day
milk group	four or more glasses of milk (Cheese, butter, or ice cream can take the place of a glass of milk.)
bread–cereal group	four or more servings
meat group	two or more servings
vegetable–fruit group	four or more servings (One citrus fruit, one green or yellow vegetable are necessary.)

ACTIVITY

Materials
paper
pencil

A. Write a breakfast, lunch, and dinner menu that includes the foods you would like to eat tomorrow.

B. Use the charts on pages 157 and 158 to find out if you have included the right amounts of food from each food group.

C. If not, rewrite your menu so that you have a balanced diet for that day.

A balanced diet is important for good health. It helps a person grow normally. It keeps the body free from un-needed fat. A balanced diet gives the body energy.

The amount of energy a food supplies is measured in units called **calories** (kal-lore-rees). Every food supplies a certain number of *calories*. Some foods supply more calories than others. For example, a tomato is about 30 calories, and a piece of chocolate cake is about 300 calories.

If you take in more calories than your body needs, you will gain weight. What do you think will happen if you take in fewer calories than your body needs?

The amount of calories a person needs depends on many things. The amount of calories needed depends on the person's age. Young people need more calories than older people. Weight, size, and whether the person is male or female also make a difference in the number of calories needed. The amount of calories needed also depends on the activity or work the person does. Would an athlete or a librarian need more energy? Who should take in more calories?

Calories: The units used to measure the amount of energy a food supplies.

MAIN IDEAS

A balanced diet includes the right amounts of all the nutrients the body needs. Foods are divided into four groups. You need a certain amount of food from each group to have a balanced diet. Every food supplies a certain number of calories.

QUESTIONS

Write your answers on a sheet of paper.

1. What word describes a diet that includes the right amounts of all the nutrients the body needs?
2. Name the four food groups and give an example of two food items in each group.
3. What units are used to measure the amount of energy a food supplies? Why do some people need to take in more calories than others?

SOMETHING EXTRA

Have you ever eaten in a restaurant? Who do you think cooked the food you ate?

A restaurant's chef is a very important person. However, chefs also prepare meals in hospitals, schools, and factories.

Most chefs are specially trained. In training, chefs learn how to prepare food by practicing in classroom kitchens. They also learn how to use and care for kitchen equipment, select and buy food, store food, use leftovers, and plan menus. Many states require that they follow sanitary rules when handling food.

Cleanliness and a good sense of smell and taste are important for a chef. Why do you think so?

CHAPTER

10

DIGESTION AND CIRCULATION

1 WHERE DOES THE FOOD GO?

Do you think the children in the picture will be able to eat their sandwiches while standing on their heads? Will the food stay on the roofs of their mouths? Or will the food go to their stomachs?

When you finish this lesson, you should be able to:

○ Name the system that changes the food you eat into a liquid.

○ Identify the parts of that system.

○ Explain why food must be changed to a liquid.

161

The children in the picture on page 161 will be able to eat their sandwiches. The food will go to their stomachs. However, it isn't wise to eat food while standing on your head. What happens to food when it is eaten? Where does the food go?

Imagine you just bit into a crisp, juicy apple. What happens to the apple inside your mouth?

Saliva: A liquid in your mouth that moistens food.

Esophagus: The tube between your mouth and stomach.

When you chew, your teeth cut, shred, and grind the apple. Your tongue moves the food around your mouth. A liquid in your mouth, called **saliva** (sa-**lie**-vah), moistens the food. When the food has been made small by the teeth and soft by the *saliva*, you swallow.

Swallowed food goes into a tube called the **esophagus** (eh-**sof**-ah-guss). The *esophagus* begins at the back of your throat and ends at your stomach. Food does not fall down the esophagus, but is pushed along. The walls of the esophagus move in a wavy motion. The motion is in one direction, toward the stomach. The food is pushed along the esophagus by the motion. Even if you stood on your head, swallowed food would be pushed in the direction of the stomach.

In the stomach, the food is churned into tiny pieces. The food is also mixed with a liquid called **gastric juice** (gas-trick). The food stays in the stomach for two to three hours. At the end of that time the churning and *gastric juice* have changed the food into a liquid. Why do you think food is changed into a liquid?

Gastric juice: A liquid in the stomach that mixes with the food.

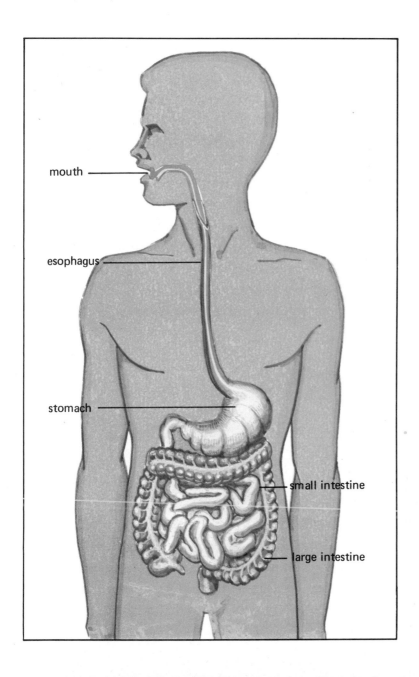

mouth

esophagus

stomach

small intestine

large intestine

Every cell in your body needs food for energy, growth, and repair. However, large pieces of solid food cannot travel through your body to every cell. The food must be changed into a liquid form that the body can use.

The liquid food moves from the stomach into the **small intestine** (in-tes-tin). The *small intestine* is a coiled tube. If the tube was stretched out, it would be 7 m (20 ft) long. Most of the liquid food passes through the wall of the small intestine. The liquid food is then carried by the blood to the cells in the body. You will learn more about this process in the next two lessons.

Not all the liquid food passes through the wall of the small intestine. Some of the liquid food goes into a larger tube at the end of the small intestine. This tube is called the **large intestine**. Water is taken out of the liquid. What remains is solid waste the body doesn't use. The solid waste leaves the body through the *large intestine*.

The mouth, esophagus, stomach, small intestine, and large intestine are parts of the **digestive system** (die-jes-tiv). The *digestive system* is a group of body parts working together to do a job. Their job is to change food into a liquid form that the body can use.

Small intestine: A long tube that food enters when the food leaves the stomach.

Large intestine: A tube that liquid waste enters.

Digestive system: The system that changes food into a liquid the body can use.

MAIN IDEAS

The digestive system changes food into a liquid form that the body can use. The mouth, esophagus, stomach, small intestine, and large intestine are parts of the system. Saliva and gastric juice are two liquids that mix with the food.

QUESTIONS

Write your answers on a sheet of paper.

1. What system changes food into a liquid form that the body can use?
2. Tell which part of the digestive system is described in each phrase below:
   a. where food is cut, ground, and moistened
   b. food is pushed through it to the stomach
   c. contains gastric juice
   d. a 7-m (20-ft) long tube
   e. a large tube at the end of the small intestine
3. Why must food be changed to a liquid?

SOMETHING EXTRA

Can you imagine looking inside a part of the human body? Doctors do when they perform surgery. However, before 1900, surgery was rarely performed. Doctors knew little about how the body parts looked and worked.

In 1822, William Beaumont, a doctor in the United States Army, was able to look inside a man's stomach. The man was Alexis St. Martin. St. Martin had a bullet wound that left a large hole in the wall of his stomach. The wound never healed properly. A large hole remained. A flap was placed over the hole to keep materials in the stomach from falling out.

For 11 years Dr. Beaumont watched how food was digested in St. Martin's stomach. The doctor saw how the stomach moved and churned food. He found out that a juice mixed with the food. Do you know what juice that is?

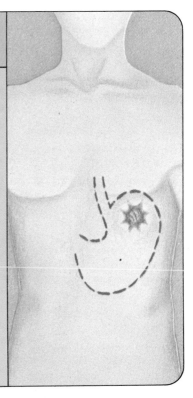

2 HOW DO THE CELLS GET FOOD?

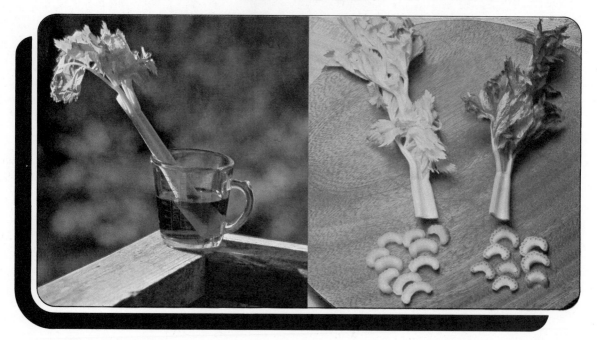

Look at the picture on the left. What do you see? Look at the picture on the right. What has happened to the celery that was in the colored water?

The pictures above were taken several hours apart. During that time, the colored water traveled up the stem of the celery to the leaves.

The leaves of a plant need water and minerals from the soil. The minerals are carried in the water through the plant to the plant's parts. The cells in your body also need food. Food is carried through your body to the cells. When you finish this lesson, you should be able to:

○ Explain how liquid food gets into the blood.

○ Name and describe the tubes through which blood flows.

○ Name the system that carries food and other materials to all the cells in the body.

Food is carried to the cells in your body by your blood. How does the food get into your blood?

The wall of your small intestine has many bumps and bulges. These bulges are called **villi** (vil-eye). The drawing below shows what the *villi* look like. Inside each villus are tiny tubes through which blood flows. Tubes through which blood flows are called **vessels** (vess-sels). The red and blue lines you see in the drawing show the blood *vessels* in the villi.

The liquid food in your small intestine passes through the walls of the villi into the blood vessels. The blood in the blood vessels carries the food to all the body cells.

Villi: Bulges in the wall of the small intestine.

Vessels: Tubes through which blood flows.

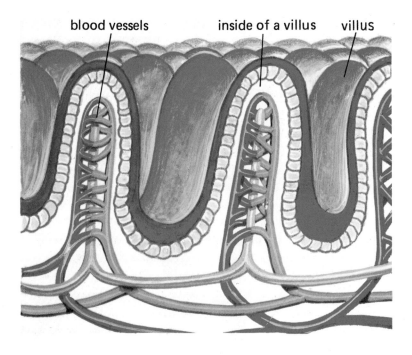

blood vessels   inside of a villus   villus

Blood is pumped around the body by the heart. Blood flows to and from the heart through blood vessels. The blood vessels that carry blood from the heart to all the parts of the body are called **arteries** (ar-ter-rees). The blood vessels that carry blood from all the parts of the body to the heart are called **veins** (vanes).

Arteries: Blood vessels that carry blood from the heart.

Veins: Blood vessels that carry blood to the heart.

Capillaries: Tiny blood vessels that connect arteries and veins.

Look at the drawing below. Can you locate the heart? Do you see the red lines? The red lines show the *arteries*. The blue lines show the *veins*. Arteries and veins are connected to each other by tiny blood vessels called **capillaries** (**kap**-pill-leh-rees). Blood flows from arteries through *capillaries* into veins.

Every cell in the body is near a capillary. The liquid food in the blood passes through the walls of the capillary into each cell. The cell uses the food for energy, growth, and repair.

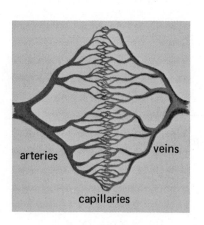

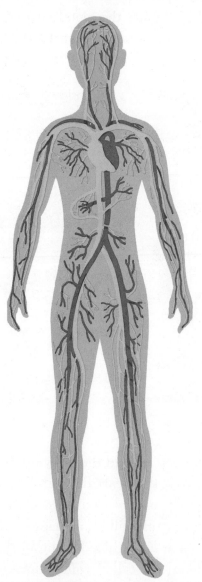

The heart, arteries, veins, and capillaries are parts of the **circulatory system** (sir-cue-la-tore-re). The job of the *circulatory system* is to carry food and other materials to all the cells in the body.

MAIN IDEAS

Liquid food passes through the walls of the small intestine. The food enters blood vessels and is carried by the blood to all the parts of the body. The heart pumps blood around the body.

QUESTIONS

Write your answers on a sheet of paper.

1. Describe how liquid food gets into the blood through the body part shown below.
2. What are blood vessels?
3. Name three blood vessels and describe each.
4. What system carries food and other materials to all the cells in the body?

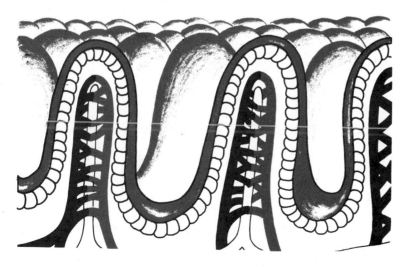

3 THE HEART

Do you know what beats about 72 times per minute and pumps about 5 liters (1.3 gallons) of blood at the same time?

If you said your heart, then you are right! Your heart is one of the most important parts of your body.

When you finish this lesson, you should be able to:

○ Describe the heart.

○ Explain the path of blood through the heart.

○ Tell how blood flows through arteries and veins.

Your heart is about the size of your fist. It is located a little to the left of the middle of your chest. Your heart is made mostly of muscle. Like all muscles, it contracts and relaxes. Each heartbeat is the sound of the heart muscle contracting.

Inside, the heart is divided into four sections. The sections at the upper part of the heart are called **atria** (ay-tree-uh). The heart has a right and left *atrium*. The sections at the lower part of the heart are called **ventricles** (ven-trih-kulls). The heart has a right and left *ventricle*.

Let us follow the path of blood through the heart. First, blood enters the right atrium, numbered 1 in the drawing at the right. Then the blood flows into the right ventricle, numbered 2 in the drawing. When the heart contracts, the blood is pushed out of the right ventricle through a large artery. The blood flows through the artery to the lungs. There, air gets into the blood. The blood flows back to the heart and enters the left atrium, numbered 3 in the drawing. Next, the blood flows into the left ventricle, numbered 4 in the drawing. When the heart contracts, the blood is pushed out of the left ventricle through another large artery. This artery branches into many smaller arteries carrying the blood to all the body parts. The blood flows back to the heart from the body parts through veins and enters the right atrium again. Then the process starts over.

Atria: The sections at the upper part of the heart.

Ventricles: The sections at the lower part of the heart.

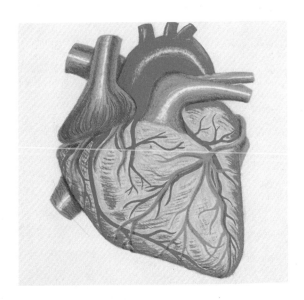

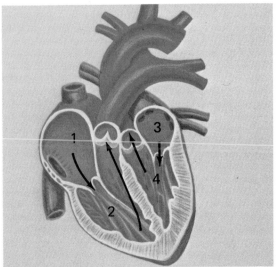

Blood does not flow smoothly through the arteries and veins. Imagine turning a water faucet on and off many times quickly. The water would come out of the faucet in spurts. As the heart contracts, the blood is pushed out of the heart in the same way. The blood flows through the blood vessels in spurts. You can feel the blood moving in this way through an artery. When this happens, you feel your **pulse (puls)**. In the following activity, you will feel and count your *pulse*. You will need a partner.

Pulse: The spurting of blood past a place in an artery.

ACTIVITY

Materials
wristwatch with
  second hand

A. Sit quietly. Place your index and middle fingers of one hand on the wrist of your other hand, as shown in the picture.

B. When you feel movement under the tips of your fingers, you are feeling your pulse.

C. Have your partner time you for 30 seconds. During the 30 seconds, count the number of times you feel your pulse.

1. What number did you count to?

D. Switch places with your partner and repeat the activity.

You felt the blood spurting through an artery that is close to the surface of your skin. Each time your heart contracted, blood spurted past the place where you held your fingers. On the average, the heart contracts 72 times per minute. This number is your pulse or heartbeat rate.

MAIN IDEAS

The heart is about the size of your fist. The heart is divided into sections called atria and ventricles. The heart is made mostly of muscle. When the muscles contract, blood is sent to all the body parts through arteries. The blood returns to the heart through veins.

QUESTIONS

Write your answers on a sheet of paper.

1. How big is your heart? Where is it located?
2. What are atria? ventricles? How many atria are there in the heart? how many ventricles?
3. Describe the path of blood through the heart, beginning with the right atrium.
4. How does the blood flow through arteries and veins?

11 RESPIRATION AND EXCRETION

1 HOW CELLS USE FOOD AND AIR

Earth is surrounded by air. Scientists believe that no other planet near the sun has the same kind of air around it as Earth does. The air around Earth is important to life on Earth. Why do you think so?

When you finish this lesson, you should be able to:

○ Name two gases in air.

○ Name a kind of sugar that one of these gases combines with.

○ Explain what happens when this sugar and gas combine.

Air is a group of many gases. Two of these gases are **oxygen** (ox-si-jen) and **carbon dioxide** (kar-bon die-ox-side). Look at the first circle chart below. It shows the percentage of each gas in the air you breathe in. What gases are in the air? The second circle chart shows the percentage of each gas in the air you breathe out. How have the percentages changed?

Oxygen: A gas in the air the body uses.

Carbon dioxide: A gas in the air given off by the body.

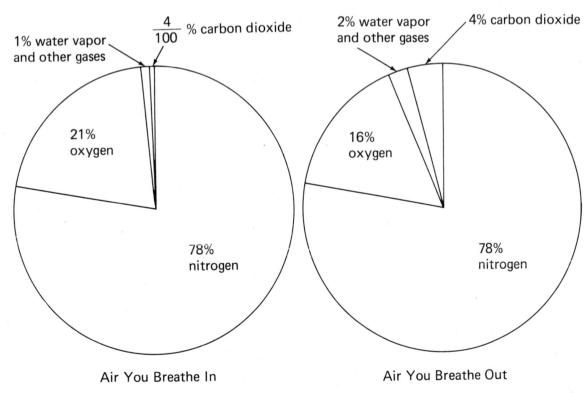

1% water vapor and other gases

$\frac{4}{100}$ % carbon dioxide

21% oxygen

78% nitrogen

Air You Breathe In

2% water vapor and other gases

4% carbon dioxide

16% oxygen

78% nitrogen

Air You Breathe Out

You breathe in more *oxygen* than you breathe out. You breathe out more *carbon dioxide* than you breathe in. What happens to the oxygen? Where does the extra carbon dioxide come from?

The oxygen you breathe in is carried by the blood to every cell in your body. The blood also carries food that is in a liquid form. In every cell, the oxygen combines with a substance in the food called **glucose** (**glue**-kose). *Glucose* is a kind of sugar. When glucose and oxygen combine, carbon dioxide, water vapor, and energy are produced. The carbon dioxide passes through the wall of the cell and goes into the blood. The blood carries the gas to your lungs, where you breathe it out. Therefore, the extra carbon dioxide you breathe out comes from the cells' use of oxygen and food. Because the cells use some of the oxygen, you breathe out less oxygen than you breathe in.

Look at the picture below. The girl is breathing out on a mirror. What do you see on the mirror?

Glucose: A kind of sugar.

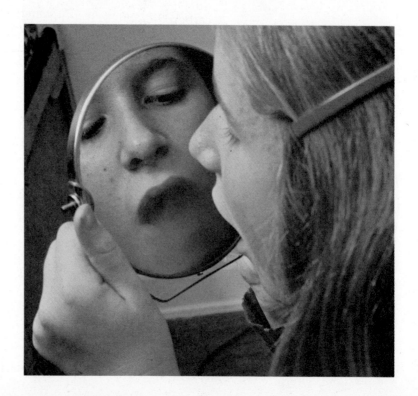

The mirror is foggy. The fog was caused by the water vapor the girl breathed out. Water is produced when oxygen and glucose combine in the cells. Some of the water left her body in the form of water vapor when she breathed out. In lesson 3 you will find out more about the removal of water from the body.

Energy is produced when glucose and oxygen combine in the cells. With this energy, the cells can grow and repair themselves.

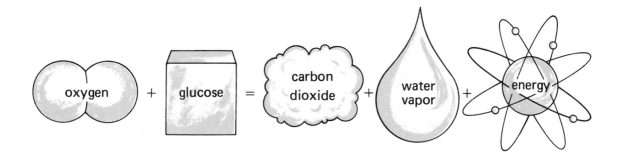

oxygen + glucose = carbon dioxide + water vapor + energy

Write your answers on a sheet of paper.

1. What are two gases in air?
2. What substance does oxygen combine with in the body's cells?
3. Why do you breathe out more carbon dioxide and less oxygen than you breathe in?
4. What words are missing from the diagram below?

oxygen + glucose = ___ + ___ + ___

SOMETHING EXTRA

A long time ago some people thought blood sloshed around inside the body. Others thought the blood flowed back and forth inside the body like the tides. It wasn't until the early 1600's that a scientist found out that blood circulated in the body. This discovery was made by William Harvey in 1628. He was the first scientist to realize that blood flowed to and from the heart through blood vessels.

Harvey was born in England in 1578. He studied medicine and became a doctor.

2 HOW DO THE CELLS GET AIR?

Sit quietly. Take a deep breath through your nose. Then breathe out. Take a deep breath through your mouth. Breathe out. What did you breathe in? Did the air you breathed in through your mouth feel different?

When you finish this lesson, you should be able to:

○ Name the system that takes in and gives off gases needed and used by the body's cells.

○ Identify some of the parts of this system.

○ Explain how and where air in the lungs enters the blood.

In the last lesson you learned that oxygen is carried to every body cell by the blood. How do you think oxygen gets into the blood?

At the beginning of this lesson you breathed air in through your nose and mouth. Inside your nose are tiny hairs and mucus. The hairs and mucus catch dirt that could enter your nose with the air. They prevent this dirt from entering your body. Also, the air is warmed in your nose. These things do not happen when you breathe in through your mouth. Did the air you breathed in through your mouth feel colder?

From your nose, air moves down the back of your throat. You are able to breathe in through your mouth or nose because both connect with your throat. The air then passes into a tube called the windpipe, or **trachea** (**tray-key-ah**). The *trachea* is also lined with tiny hairs. These hairs catch dirt. When you cough or sneeze, the dirt is pushed up and out of the trachea. The dirt leaves the body through the mouth.

The trachea divides into two parts called **bronchi** (**bron-**key). Each *bronchus* goes into a lung. You have a left lung and right lung. Inside the lungs, the bronchi divide many times and branch into many small tubes.

Trachea: The windpipe at the back of the throat.

Bronchi: Branches of the trachea.

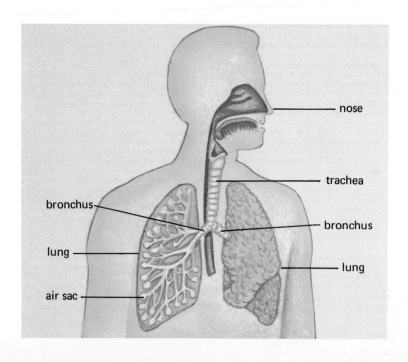

180

Look at the diagram on page 180. Can you find the trachea, bronchi, and small tubes?

At the end of the many small tubes in the lungs are groups of tiny balloon-shaped sacs called **air sacs.** Look at the drawing on the right. It shows a group of *air sacs.* Around the air sacs are many capillaries.

When you breathe in, air flows into the trachea, then travels through the many branches of the bronchi into the air sacs. The walls of the air sacs are very thin. So are the walls of the capillaries. Air passes through the walls of the air sacs into the blood in the capillaries. The blood returns to the heart, carrying the needed oxygen. From the heart, the blood is pumped to all of the body cells.

In the cells a kind of exchange occurs. Oxygen and food leave the blood and enter the cells. Carbon dioxide and water leave the cells and enter the blood. The blood carries the carbon dioxide and water back to the lungs. There, these substances enter the air sacs. When you breathe out, the carbon dioxide and water are pushed out through the bronchi, trachea, and nose.

Air sacs: Groups of balloon-shaped sacs in the lungs.

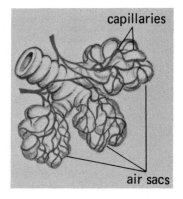

capillaries

air sacs

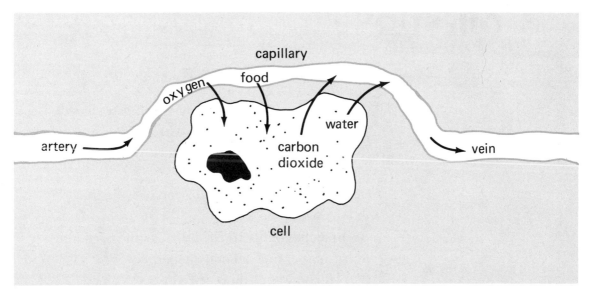

capillary

oxygen

food

water

artery

carbon dioxide

vein

cell

**Respiratory system:
The system that takes
in and gives off gases.**

Your nose, trachea, bronchi, lungs, and air sacs are some parts of your **respiratory system** (res-pu-rah-tore-ee). The job of your *respiratory system* is to take in and give off gases needed and used by the body cells.

MAIN IDEAS

The nose, trachea, bronchi, lungs, and air sacs are parts of your body that take in and give off gases. The body takes in more oxygen than it gives off. Oxygen is used by the body cells.

QUESTIONS

Write your answers on a sheet of paper.

1. What system takes in and gives off gases needed and used by the body cells?
2. Name the part of the respiratory system described in each phrase below:
   a. warms and cleans the air you breathe in
   b. the windpipe
   c. branches of the trachea that go into each lung
   d. groups of tiny balloon-shaped sacs
3. Explain how and where air enters the blood.

3 GETTING RID OF WASTES

The oil that flows through the engine of a car gets dirty. The engine has a part that cleans the dirty oil. Do you know the name of that car part? A car's oil filter removes dirt from the oil. The oil that leaves the oil filter is clean.

The blood carries substances that the body doesn't need. These substances are wastes. Your body has a part that removes these wastes and cleans your blood.

When you finish this lesson, you should be able to:

○ Name the system that removes wastes from the blood.

○ Identify some of the parts of this system.

○ Explain how wastes are removed from the blood.

Kidneys: Parts of your body that remove wastes from the blood.

Have you ever seen beans like the ones in the picture? Do you know the name for these beans? These beans have the same shape as parts of your body called **kidneys** (**kid**-nees). You have two *kidneys*. They are larger than kidney beans. They are about the size of your fist. Your kidneys are at about the middle of your back, near your backbone.

Your kidneys are like the oil filter in a car. They remove wastes from the blood.

ACTIVITY

Materials
dirty water
glass jar
paper cup
paper towel
rubber band

A. Place the paper towel over the empty jar as shown. Fasten the towel with the rubber band.

B. Slowly pour the dirty water from the cup into the jar.

1. What is on the paper towel?

2. How is the water in the jar different from the water that was in the cup?

The paper towel acted as a filter. It removed the dirt from the water. The water in the jar was clean.

Each kidney in your body has 1,250,000 tiny filters. These filters are called **nephrons** (**nef**-frons). There are many tiny capillaries around the *nephrons.*

Nephrons: Tiny filters in the kidneys.

Blood enters the kidneys through arteries and flows into the tiny capillaries. At this point, the blood contains wastes. The wastes contain mostly water. The wastes are removed in the nephrons. The clean blood flows back to the heart. The wastes leave the kidneys through two long tubes called **ureters** (**yur**-ret-ters). Look at the diagram. Can you find the *ureters?*

Ureters: Two long tubes through which wastes leave the kidneys.

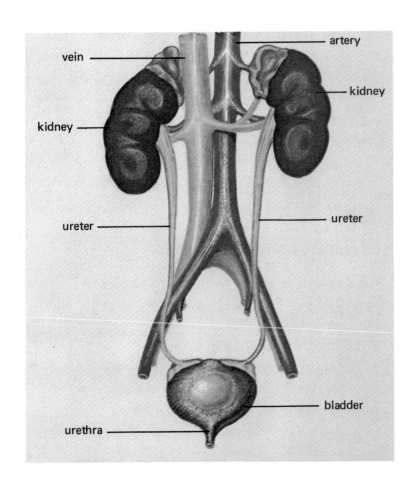

Bladder: A part of the body in which urine is stored.

Urethra: Part of the body through which urine leaves the body.

Excretory system: The system that removes wastes from the body.

The ureters connect the kidneys to the **bladder** (**blad**-er). The waste, now called urine, is stored in the *bladder*. The bladder is a muscle-lined sac. When it contracts, the urine is pushed out of the body through the **urethra** (you-**reeth**-rah). Can you find the *urethra* in the diagram on page 186?

Your kidneys, ureters, bladder, and urethra are some parts of your **excretory system** (ex-kreh-tore-ee). The job of your *excretory system* is to remove wastes from the blood.

MAIN IDEAS

Your blood contains wastes that must be removed. The kidneys, ureters, bladder, and urethra are some parts of your body that remove these wastes from your blood.

QUESTIONS

Write your answers on a sheet of paper.

1. What system removes wastes from the blood?
2. Name the part of your excretory system described in each phrase below:
   a. located near your backbone
   b. the filters in the kidneys
   c. tubes that connect the kidneys and bladder
   d. stores urine
   e. part through which urine passes out of the body
3. How are wastes removed from the blood?

12 TAKING CARE OF YOURSELF

1 TOBACCO

The picture above shows a machine that smokes cigarette tobacco. It can smoke over 10 cigarettes at one
time. Scientists use this smoking machine to find out
about the effects of tobacco smoking.

When you finish this lesson, you should be able to:

○ Tell how smoking tobacco affects the heart.

○ Explain what happens to parts of a smoker's
respiratory system.

Smoking tobacco is a dangerous habit. Poisonous substances in tobacco, such as tar and nicotine, can cause harm to the body systems.

The heart and the lungs are two body parts that can be damaged by smoking. The heart of a smoker beats 10,000 times more a day than that of a nonsmoker. Therefore, the heart of a smoker must work harder than it should.

Heart disease is the greatest cause of death in the United States. Look at the chart below. The chance of getting heart disease is about 100 percent greater for smokers than for nonsmokers. It is believed that every cigarette shortens a smoker's life by five and one half minutes.

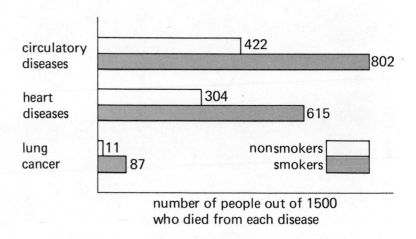

number of people out of 1500
who died from each disease

In your lungs, cigarette smoke, tar, and nicotine can cause many problems. The bronchus and its many small branches get clogged. The tiny hairs in the trachea can be destroyed, allowing dirt and other substances to enter the lungs. The air sacs can become broken or clogged. There are more cases of lung cancer and other respiratory diseases among smokers than among nonsmokers. Look at the two pictures on the next page. The one on the top shows the healthy lung of a nonsmoker. The one on the bottom shows the lung of a smoker. How are the lungs different?

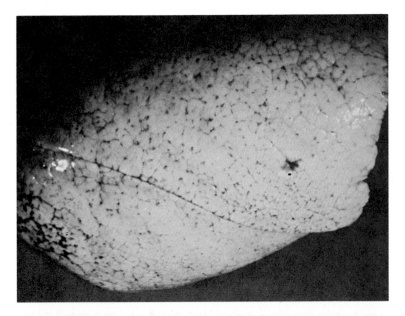

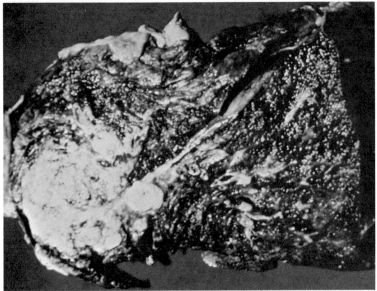

Some people believe they will not have these lung problems if they do not breathe in the tobacco smoke. These people smoke cigars or pipes. However, cancers of the mouth, throat, and esophagus are common among cigar and pipe smokers.

It is believed that 75 percent of all smokers started smoking tobacco before they were twenty years of age.

ACTIVITY

Materials
paper
pencil

A. Number your paper from 1 to 5.

B. Read each numbered statement on the chart below. Then, next to the proper number on your paper, write whether you agree, neither agree nor disagree, or disagree with each statement.

C. Ask members of your family what they think about each statement.

statements	do you: agree	neither agree or disagree	disagree
1. Smoking is a bad habit.	?	?	?
2. It is okay to smoke only five cigarettes a day.	?	?	?
3. If you are healthy, smoking tobacco will not harm you.	?	?	?
4. It is difficult to stop smoking tobacco.	?	?	?
5. The smoking habit costs more money than the price of a pack of cigarettes, cigars, or pipe tobacco.	?	?	?

Why do you think people start to smoke even though they know it is dangerous? Many people know smoking is dangerous but don't think they will become ill. Also, some people smoke because their friends do. Do you?

There is a warning on every pack of cigarettes. Look at the picture of the cigarette pack on the next page. What is the warning?

MAIN IDEAS

Smoking tobacco can cause damage to the body systems. Heart and lung disease are more common among smokers than nonsmokers.

QUESTIONS

Write your answers on a sheet of paper.

1. How does smoking tobacco affect the heart?
2. What happens to the bronchi, trachea, and air sacs of a smoker?
3. How do the lungs of a smoker look different from the lungs of a nonsmoker?

2 ALCOHOL AND DRUGS

In many states the legal drinking age is twenty-one. Do you know what that means? In these states alcohol cannot be sold to persons under twenty-one years of age. However drinking a great amount of alcohol is not safe or wise for persons over that age.

When you finish this lesson, you should be able to:

○ Tell how alcohol affects the body cells, heart, and stomach.

○ Tell how drugs affect heartbeat and breathing.

When you eat, food stays in the digestive system for about three hours. Then the liquid food enters the blood. When a person drinks alcohol, the alcohol enters the blood in two minutes. The blood carries the alcohol to every cell in the body.

The amount of alcohol in a person's blood can be measured by testing a blood sample taken from that person. The amount of alcohol is shown as a percent. One tenth of one percent (0.1%) or higher is a harmful amount of alcohol in the blood. Tests can also be made on a urine or breath sample to find out the amount of alcohol in the body. The person in the picture below is taking an alcohol breath test.

The amount of alcohol that enters a person's blood depends on two things. First, the person's weight and second, the number of drinks the person takes in.

ACTIVITY

Materials
none

A. Using the chart below, answer the following questions:

1. A person who weighs 45 kg (100 lb) has four drinks in one hour. What is the percentage of alcohol in that person's blood?

2. A 90-kg (200-lb) person has four drinks in one hour. What is the percentage of alcohol in that person's blood?

number of drinks in one hour	body weight in kilograms (pounds)							
	45 (100)	54 (120)	63 (140)	72 (160)	81 (180)	90 (200)	99 (220)	108 (240)
1	.04	.03	.03	.02	.02	.02	.02	.02
2	.08	.06	.05	.05	.04	.04	.03	.03
3	.11	.09	.08	.07	.06	.06	.05	.05
4	.15	.12	.11	.09	.08	.08	.07	.06
5	.19	.16	.13	.12	.11	.09	.09	.08
6	.23	.19	.16	.14	.13	.11	.10	.09
7	.26	.22	.19	.16	.15	.13	.12	.11
8	.30	.25	.21	.19	.17	.15	.14	.13
9	.34	.28	.24	.21	.19	.17	.15	.14
10	.38	.31	.27	.23	.21	.19	.17	.16

percentages of alcohol
in blood

Two people can have the same number of alcoholic drinks. However, the amount of alcohol in the blood can be different if the weights of the two people are very different.

194

Alcohol in the cells produces heat. This raises the temperature of the blood. The person gets an untrue feeling of warmth and might go outdoors in very cold weather without the proper clothing. Why might this be harmful to the person?

Alcohol in the cells also produces a great amount of water. The blood carries the water to the kidneys. This causes a great amount of water to collect in the kidneys. The result can be kidney damage.

A person who drinks a great deal of alcohol may not eat the right amount of food. How do you think this affects the body? Will this person get the nutrients necessary for good health? In an empty stomach, alcohol may cause the walls of the stomach to swell. The person will feel pain and discomfort.

Early Bird Warning Signs of Alcoholism

Difficult to get along with when drinking.

Lies about drinking.

Neglects to eat when drinking.

Alcohol slows the action of the heart, or the number of times the heart beats in one minute. As a result, the blood supply to the cells is slowed. The cells do not get oxygen and food as fast as they are needed.

Drugs can also harm the body systems. Some people take drugs for reasons that are not medical. The drugs can increase or decrease their heartbeat and breathing rates. This can be very dangerous. A person's heartbeat and breathing may be slowed so much that they stop.

Do you know anyone who sniffs glue? Some people breathe in glue, paint thinner, or kerosene because they think it makes them feel good. However, the fumes from these substances can damage their lungs. Also, the fumes enter the blood and take the place of oxygen needed by all the body cells.

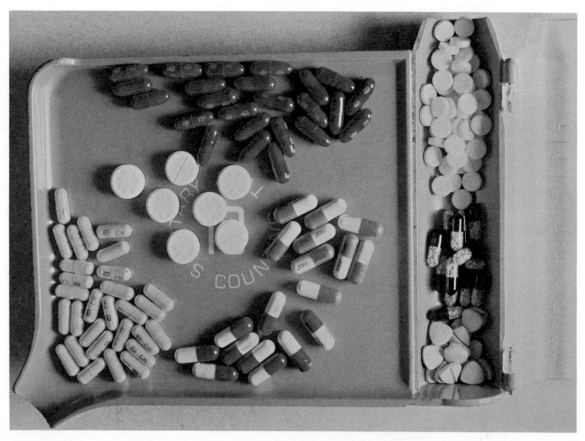

Alcohol and drugs can be harmful to the body systems. Alcohol enters the blood within two minutes after it is swallowed. The blood carries the alcohol to every cell in the body. Drugs can affect a person's heartbeat and breathing.

QUESTIONS

Write your answers on a sheet of paper.

1. How long does alcohol take to enter the blood?
2. Tell how alcohol affects each of the following:
   a. the body cells
   b. the heart
   c. the stomach
3. What can happen to the heartbeat and breathing of people who take drugs that speed them up or slow them down?

SOMETHING EXTRA

Alcoholism is not a habit. It is a disease. Many hospitals and health care centers have programs for treating this disease.

In 1935, a group called **Alcoholics Anonymous** (al-ko-**hoi**-licks ah-**non**-eh-mus) was started. *Alcoholics Anonymous* is a group of people with drinking problems who try to help one another. The group has meetings at which the members discuss their disease and how they can live better lives without alcohol.

Since 1965, Alcoholics Anonymous has had over 1,000,000 members. There are 40,000 groups in 92 countries.

Foods contain nutrients. Nutrients are chemicals that your body needs for growth, repair, and energy.

The digestive system changes food into a liquid form that the body can use. The mouth, esophagus, stomach, small intestine, and large intestine are some parts of the digestive system. The circulatory system carries food and other materials in the blood to all the cells in the body. The heart, arteries, veins, and capillaries are parts of the circulatory system. Other materials carried by the blood are oxygen, carbon dioxide, wastes, and water.

The respiratory system takes in and gives off gases. The nose, trachea, bronchi, lungs, and air sacs are parts of the respiratory system. The excretory system removes wastes, such as water, from the blood. The kidneys, ureters, bladder, and urethra are some parts of the excretory system.

The use of tobacco, alcohol, and drugs can be harmful to the body systems.

CHECK YOURSELF

1. What are nutrients? Name six nutrients and list examples of food sources for each nutrient.
2. What is a balanced diet?
3. Name the food group each of the following food items belongs to.
   a. ice cream   **c.** apple
   b. steak   **d.** spaghetti
4. What is a calorie?
5. What is the job of your digestive system?
6. Explain the path of food through your digestive system.

7. How does liquid food enter the blood?
8. Describe the flow of blood through the four sections of the heart. Name these sections of the heart.
9. What is the job of each of the following?
   a. heart   **c.** veins
   b. arteries   **d.** capillaries
10. What two substances combine in the body cells and produce carbon dioxide, water, and energy?
11. Describe the path of air from your nose to your blood.
12. What are nephrons? Where are they located?
13. Describe the parts of your excretory system.
14. How does smoking tobacco affect the heart and lungs?
15. What are three effects of alcohol on the body? two effects of drugs?

PROJECTS

1. Get a piece of brown wrapping paper as long as you are tall. Also, get a friend to help you. Place the paper on the floor and tape the ends of the paper to the floor. Lie down on the paper on your back, with your head turned to the side. Have your friend draw the outline of your body. Within your outline, you can draw the position of the parts of one of your body systems. You can draw in the parts of your digestive, circulatory, respiratory, or excretory system. Label the parts. If you wish, color them with crayons or paint.

2. How does exercise affect your heartbeat or pulse? You may need a friend to time you while you are doing this project. Sit quietly and take your pulse for 30 seconds. Write your pulse on a sheet of paper. Then do one of the following: jump rope for 30 seconds, walk up and down steps for 30 seconds, bounce a ball while running 12 m (40 ft) and back. Then quickly sit down and take your pulse again. How has your pulse changed?

The place shown in the picture on the right is called Stonehenge. Stonehenge is in England. It is believed to be an ancient observatory. An observatory is a place where people study the objects in space.

You probably are wondering how this group of stones could help people study distant objects. Long ago, the stones formed a circle. The positions of the stones showed where the sun and moon appeared to rise and set at different times of the year. Many of the stones have been worn down by wind and water. Some fell and were taken away.

The place shown in the picture on the left is the Kitt Peak National Observatory. It is a modern observatory. The scientists at Kitt Peak use instruments to study distant objects the people at Stonehenge didn't have.

In this unit you will learn about many of the distant objects in space and the instruments used to study them.

UNIT
5
EXPLORING THE UNIVERSE

CHAPTER 13

THE EARTH
AND
THE MOON

1 DAYTIME, NIGHTTIME, AND SEASONS

What time of the day is it now? Is the sky bright or dark? How will the sky look twelve hours from now? Why do you think a change occurs?

When you finish this lesson, you should be able to:

○ Tell how Earth moves in space.

○ Explain how Earth's movements cause daytime, nighttime, and seasons.

Earth is a **planet.** A *planet* is a solid body in space that does not give off its own light. Earth gets its light from the sun.

Earth is shaped like a ball. Therefore, only the half of Earth that faces the sun gets light. Places on the half that is lit have daytime. Places on the other half are dark and have nighttime.

Earth moves in space. It spins, or **rotates** (**row**-tates). Do you feel the movement? Earth makes one complete *rotation* in 24 hours. This amount of time is called a day. Within 24 hours, or one day, most places on Earth have a daytime and a nighttime.

Earth rotates from west to east. That is why the sun seems to rise in the east and set in the west.

Planet: A solid body in space that does not give off its own light.

Rotate: To spin.

Earth also **revolves** (ree-**volvs**), or moves around, the sun. Earth makes one complete *revolution* around the sun every 365¼ days. This amount of time is called a year. Within one year, most places on Earth have four seasons. Can you name them?

Earth tilts toward or away from the sun at different times of the year.

Revolve: To move around something.

Summer soltice: The first day of summer in the Northern Hemisphere.

Winter solstice: The first day of winter in the Northern Hemisphere.

Vernal equinox: The first day of spring in the Northern Hemisphere.

Autumnal equinox: The first day of fall in the Northern Hemisphere.

On June 21, Earth's North Pole is tilted toward the sun. In the Northern Hemisphere, this is the first day of summer. June 21 is called the **summer solstice** (**sole**-stis).

On December 22, Earth's North Pole is tilted away from the sun. In the Northern Hemisphere, this is the first day of winter. December 22 is called the **winter solstice** (**sole**-stis). Look at the diagram below. Can you find the position of Earth at the *summer solstice* and *winter solstice*?

In the spring and fall, Earth is not tilted toward or away from the sun. In the Northern Hemisphere, March 21 is the first day of spring, or the **vernal equinox** (**ver**-nal **ee**-kwi-noks). The first day of fall in the Northern Hemisphere, September 23, is called the **autumnal equinox** (awe-**tum**-nal **ee**-kwi-noks). Look at the diagram again. What is the position of Earth at the *vernal equinox* and *autumnal equinox*?

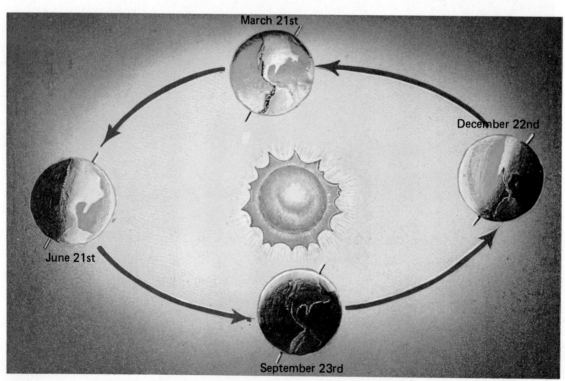

March 21st

December 22nd

June 21st

September 23rd

How is a summer's day different from a winter's day? Why do you think the days are hotter and longer in the summer than in the winter? This activity may help you find out.

A. Place one sheet of paper on your desk. Hold the lit flashlight over the paper as shown in the first picture below.

B. With the chalk draw a line around the lit area.

C. Place the other sheet of paper on your desk. Hold the lit flashlight over the paper as shown in the second picture. Then draw a line around the lit area.

1. How are the circles formed by the lines you drew different from each other?

Materials
chalk
flashlight
2 sheets of black
  construction paper

When the light shone directly on the paper, the light covered a small area. When the light shone at a slant on the paper, the light covered a larger area. Direct light is stronger than light shining at a slant because direct light is concentrated on a smaller area.

The way the light from the flashlight shone on the paper is similar to how the sun's light shines on Earth. In the summer, the sun's light shines directly on the Northern Hemisphere because of the way in which Earth is tilted toward the sun at that time of year. Look at the diagram below. In summer, Earth is tilted toward the sun. The direct light on the Northern Hemisphere is strong because the light is concentrated on a small area. The strong light heats the area.

In the winter, the sun's light shines at a slant on the Northern Hemisphere because Earth is tilted away from the sun. The slanted light is weak because it is spread out over a larger area. The weak light does not heat the area as much as strong, direct light.

In the spring and fall the sun's light is neither strong nor weak. How are spring and fall days different from summer and winter days?

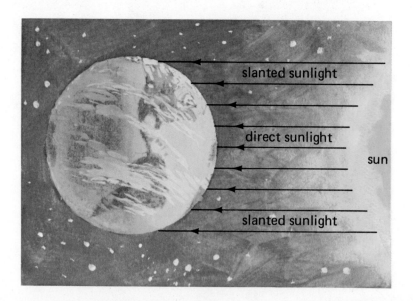

In the summer there are more hours of daylight than in the winter. What effect do you think this has on the amount of heat in the Northern Hemisphere?

When Earth is tilted toward the sun, the North Pole has 24 hours of daylight because the North Pole always faces the sun at that time. What do you think happens to the number of daylight hours at the North Pole when Earth is tilted away from the sun?

MAIN IDEAS

Earth rotates and also revolves around the sun. Earth makes one complete rotation in 24 hours. Earth makes one complete revolution in $365\frac{1}{4}$ days. Daytime, nighttime, and seasons are caused by Earth's movement.

QUESTIONS

Write your answers on a sheet of paper.

1. How does Earth move in space?
2. What movement of Earth takes $365\frac{1}{4}$ days?
3. Why do most places on Earth have a daytime and nighttime?
4. Why does the sun's light shine directly on Earth at the summer solstice and on a slant at the winter solstice?
5. Why are summer days hotter than winter days?

2 THE MOON

Have you ever heard someone say "The moon is made of green cheese"? Do you think that is true? What do you think the moon is made of?

When you finish this lesson, you should be able to:

○ Describe the surface of the moon.

○ Explain why the moon seems to change shape.

○ Tell how the moon and Earth can block the sun's light.

The moon is a solid body in space, but it is not a planet. The moon is a **satellite** (sat-tell-lite). A *satellite* is an object in space that revolves around a planet. The moon makes one complete revolution around Earth in $27\frac{1}{3}$ days.

Satellite: An object in space that revolves around a planet.

The surface of the moon is not made of green cheese. It is made of rocks and soillike materials. The moon's surface is covered with **craters** (kray-ters). *Craters* are bowl-shaped holes on the moon's surface. Look at the first picture. It shows a crater on the moon. Scientists believe the moon's craters were formed when materials traveling in space hit and dented the moon's surface.

Smooth places on the moon's surface are called **marias** (**mar**-ee-ahs). Look at the second picture. It shows a *maria* on the moon that scientists named the **Sea of Serenity** (sir-**ren**-it-tee). Another maria on the moon was named the **Sea of Tranquility** (tran-**kwil**-it-tee). Scientists have also given names to some of the moon's craters. One of the craters is named **Copernicus** (ko-**purr**-nih-kus), another is **Tycho** (**tie**-ko). There are also mountains on the moon's surface.

Probably you have seen the moon many times. Does the moon always look the same to you? How does the moon change?

Craters: Bowl-shaped holes.

Marias: Smooth places on the moon's surface.

Sea of Serenity, Sea of Tranquility: The names given to marias on the moon's surface.

Copernicus, Tycho: The names given to craters on the moon.

ACTIVITY

Materials
lamp
orange

A. Imagine that the lamp is the sun, the orange is the moon, and you are Earth.

B. Place the lamp on a table so that it is level with your eye. You may need to place books under the lamp. Turn the lamp on. Stand about 60 cm (2 ft) from the lamp. Face the lamp.

C. Hold the orange up, half way between the lamp and your eyes.

1. How much of the orange's lit surface can you see?

D. Turn so that your side faces the lamp.

E. Hold the orange up about 25 cm (10 in.) from your eyes.

2. How much of the orange's lit surface can you see?

F. Turn so that your back is facing the lamp. Hold the orange up about 25 cm (10 in.) from your eyes, but slightly to the left of your head.

3. How much of the orange's lit surface can you see?

In the activity the light was always shining on one half of the orange. However, you could not always see the whole lit surface. The first time you could not see the lit surface at all. The second time you saw only half of the lit surface. The other half was facing away from you. The third time you saw the whole lit surface. The way we see the moon is very similar.

The sun's light is always shining on half of the moon's surface. However, the whole lit surface is not always seen from Earth. As a result the moon seems to change shape. When the whole lit surface is seen, the moon looks like a round disc in the sky. This is called a full moon. Sometimes only half of the moon's lit surface is seen. This is called a half moon. Sometimes an even smaller part of the lit surface is all that can be seen. This is called a crescent moon. When the moon's lit surface cannot be seen at all, the moon is called a new moon. These apparent shapes of the moon are its **phases** (**fay**-zez). The full moon, half moon, crescent moon, and new moon are the *phases* of the moon.

Phases: The shapes the moon appears to be.

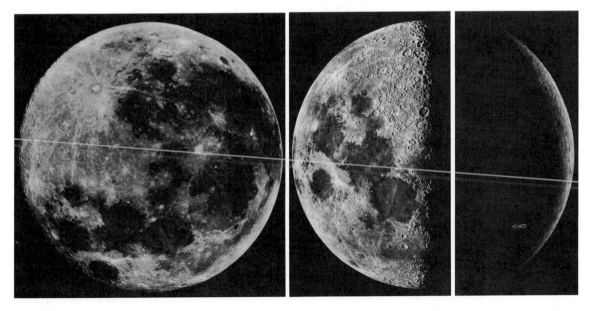

Solar eclipse: Occurs when the moon passes between Earth and the sun.

The moon revolves around Earth at the same time that Earth revolves around the sun. Sometimes the moon passes between Earth and the sun, and the moon blocks the sun's light. When this happens, a shadow of the moon is cast on Earth. This is called a **solar eclipse** (so-lar ee-**klips**). Look at the first diagram below. The *solar eclipse* can only be seen from the area on Earth where the moon's shadow falls. Can you find that area on Earth in the diagram?

Sometimes Earth passes between the moon and the sun, and Earth blocks the sun's light. When this happens a shadow of Earth is cast on the moon and the moon cannot be seen from Earth. This is called a **lunar eclipse** (**loo**-nar ee-**klips**). Look at the second diagram below. It shows the positions of the moon, Earth, and sun during a *lunar eclipse.*

Lunar eclipse: Occurs when Earth passes between the moon and the sun.

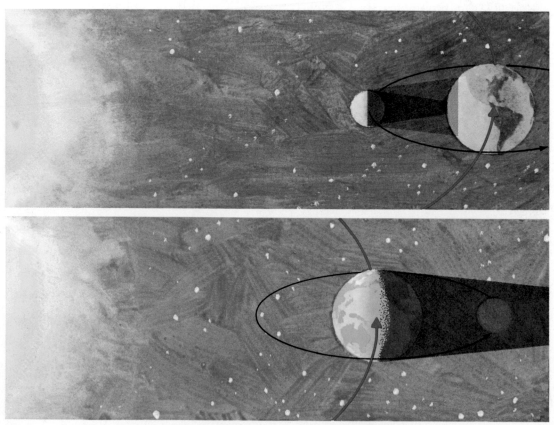

The moon is a satellite of Earth. The surface of the moon has craters, mountains, and marias. The moon seems to change shape. These apparent shapes are called the phases of the moon. At certain times, solar and lunar eclipses can occur.

QUESTIONS

Write your answers on a sheet of paper.

1. How are the moon's craters and marias different from each other? Name two of each.
2. Why does the moon seem to change shape?
3. Name four phases of the moon. Which phase cannot be seen from Earth?
4. What happens during a solar eclipse? a lunar eclipse?

SOMETHING EXTRA

The sight shown in the picture at the right is called the Northern Lights. The Northern Lights are a glowing or flickering of natural light. The lights can be seen in the night sky only from the Northern Hemisphere. In the Southern Hemisphere, the Southern Lights are seen. When the lights occur, they disappear and reappear in the same place every few seconds. This makes the lights appear to flicker. They are usually yellow-green in color, but may also appear red.

Scientists believe the Northern Lights occur when particles from the sun travel through space and strike air particles in the layer of air around Earth. The light effect occurs over 110 km (70 mi) above Earth's surface.

CHAPTER  14

THE SOLAR SYSTEM

1 THE INNER PLANETS

The crowd at the space control center cheered as a picture appeared on the television screen. *Viking I* had landed safely. For the first time, scientists were able to closely see the surface of another planet. Have you ever heard of *Viking I*? Do you know where it landed?

When you finish this lesson, you should be able to:

○ Tell the name given to the group of nine planets, their moons, and the sun.

○ Identify the four inner planets.

214

Earth is not the only planet in space. Nine planets revolve around the sun. This group of nine planets, their moons, and the sun is called our **solar system**.

The planets revolve around the sun on almost circular paths called **orbits** (or-bits). Look at the drawing below. It shows the *orbits* of the nine planets in our *solar system*. The word *solar* means *of or about the sun*. Why do you think this group of planets and moons is called the solar system?

The planets are always in the same order from the sun. The four planets closest to the sun are **Mercury** (mur-kur-rhee), **Venus** (vee-nus), **Earth**, and **Mars** (marz). They are called the inner planets. Can you find the inner planets on the drawing?

Solar system: The nine planets, their moons, and the sun.

Orbit: The path of an object in space around another.

Mercury, Venus, Earth, Mars: The four planets closest to the sun.

Mercury is the smallest planet. It is also the closest to the sun. The surface temperature on the side of Mercury facing the sun can be as high as 500°C (932°F). The surface temperature on the dark side can be −200°C (−328°F). Pictures taken by spacecrafts sent to Mercury show a surface like that of the moon. As you can see in the first picture below, Mercury has craters. Scientists believe that there is no air, water, or life on Mercury. The planet has no moons.

Venus is the second planet from the sun. It is the closest planet to *Earth*. Venus has often been called Earth's twin. Both planets are about the same size. Both planets are covered with clouds. However, there is no water on Venus, and its air is almost all carbon dioxide. Also, the surface temperature on Venus is usually 500°C (932°F). The temperature on Earth is never that high. On Venus, the sun seems to rise in the west and set in the east. On Earth the opposite occurs. This is because Venus and Earth rotate in opposite directions. Venus has no moons.

The third planet from the sun is Earth. Scientists believe Earth is the only planet that has water and air containing oxygen. Therefore, they think it is the only planet in our solar system that has life as we know it. Earth has one moon.

Mars is the fourth planet from the sun. It is about half the size of Earth. Mars appears to be red except for white spots at its poles. Scientists believe these white spots are ice caps. Look at the picture of Mars below on the left. Do you see an ice cap? The ice cap seems to get smaller during Mars' summer. Perhaps the ice melts. Most of the surface has mountains and craters. There is no water on Mars. Its air is mostly carbon dioxide and the ice caps are solid carbon dioxide. During the day on Mars, the surface temperature on the planet usually does not rise higher than 0°C (32°F). At night the surface temperature may drop to −100°C (−212°F). Why do you think the temperature is colder on Mars than on Earth? Mars has two moons.

 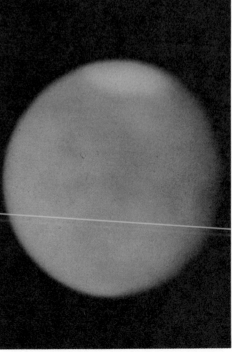

The *Viking I* spacecraft was sent to the planet Mars. Metal arms attached to the spacecraft scooped up rocks and sand. Some of the rocks look like hard sponges because they have many holes in them. Scientists believe the rocks were once in a liquid form. As they hardened to solid rock, air bubbles made the holes in the rocks.

MAIN IDEAS

Nine planets and their moons revolve around the sun. The planets revolve in almost circular orbits. The four planets closest to the sun are called the inner planets of the solar system.

QUESTIONS

Write your answers on a sheet of paper.

1. What name is given to the nine planets, their moons, and the sun?
2. Name the four inner planets.
3. Which planet is described in each phrase below?
   a. a red planet with ice caps
   b. closest planet to the sun
   c. the same size as Earth
   d. has one moon
   e. has surface temperatures of 500°C (932°F), and −200°C (−328°F).
   f. has water and air containing oxygen

2 THE OUTER PLANETS

Galileo lived a long time ago. He was a scientist who studied the planets, moon, sun, and stars. In 1610 he discovered four objects moving around the largest planet in our solar system. Do you know what the objects were? Do you know which planet in our solar system is the largest?

When you finish this lesson, you should be able to:

○ Identify the outer planets of the solar system.

○ Compare the speeds at which the planets revolve and rotate.

The five planets farthest from the sun are called the outer planets. **Jupiter** (**joo**-pit-ter), **Saturn** (sat-turn), **Uranus** (you-**ray**-nus), **Neptune** (**nep**-tune), and **Pluto** (plu-**toe**) are the outer planets.

Jupiter, Saturn, Uranus, Neptune, Pluto: The five planets farthest from the sun.

Jupiter is the largest planet in our solar system. Thirteen hundred Earths would be needed to make a planet the size of Jupiter. Jupiter is covered by bands of clouds. Look at the picture of Jupiter at the left. Do you see a giant spot on the planet? Scientists think this spot on Jupiter may be a large and long-lasting storm. The spot is believed to be as wide as Earth and 13 times as long. There is no water on Jupiter.

The objects that Galileo saw moving around Jupiter were its moons. Galileo saw only four of Jupiter's 14 moons.

The second largest planet in our solar system is *Saturn*. It is the next planet from the sun after Jupiter. Saturn is also covered with clouds. Look at the picture below. What do you see around the planet? Saturn is famous for its four rings. The rings extend out into space around the planet. Scientists believe the rings are made of millions of small particles. Saturn has 10 moons. One moon is the size of Mercury.

The next planet from the sun is *Uranus*. It is so far away that little information is known about the planet. Uranus is about half the size of Jupiter and Saturn. However, it is a giant compared to Earth. Uranus has rings like Saturn. Uranus has five rings. Scientists are not sure about the makeup of these rings. The planet has five moons.

Beyond Uranus are the planets *Neptune* and *Pluto*. Very little is known about them. They are too far away to see very clearly. Neptune is about the same size as Uranus. Pluto probably is the size of Mercury. Neptune has two moons. Scientists are not sure if Pluto has moons.

ACTIVITY

Materials
basketball
clay
meterstick

A. The chart below lists the nine planets. It also lists scale numbers to use in making a solar system model.

B. For each planet make a ball of clay that measures across the number shown on the chart for that planet.

C. When all the planet models are complete, go outside to the schoolyard with the models.

D. Have a classmate stand at one end of the yard and hold the basketball. The basketball represents the sun. Have another classmate stand 12 m (40 ft) from the "sun" and hold up the Mercury model.

E. Measure the distances for each planet shown on the chart that will fit within your schoolyard.

planet	model scale	distance scale
Mercury	1 mm	12 m
Venus	2 mm	22 m
Earth	2 mm	30 m
Mars	1 mm	46 m
Jupiter	28 mm	155 m
Saturn	26 mm	285 m
Uranus	10 mm	574 m
Neptune	9 mm	899 m
Pluto	1 mm	1,191 m

In the activity you made a model of the solar system. Which planet was the largest? the smallest? Which planet was farthest from the sun? Which planet was closest to the sun? If you had a distance scale in which 20 cm (8 in.) = 1,000,000 km (620,000 mi) for the distance of each planet from the sun, you would have to set up your model on a football field.

Below is a chart showing the real distance of each planet from the sun and the number of days it takes each planet to revolve and rotate. The planets revolve and rotate at different speeds. Which planet takes the most time to revolve around the sun? Which planet rotates the slowest?

planet	distance from sun in millions of km (mi)	rotation time	revolution time
Mercury	58 (36)	58 days 18 hr	88 days
Venus	108 (67)	247 days	224.7 days
Earth	150 (93)	23 hr 56 min	365.2 days
Mars	228 (141)	24 hr 37 min	687 days
Jupiter	778 (482)	9 hr 50 min	11.86 years
Saturn	1,430 (887)	10 hr 14 min	29.46 years
Uranus	2,870 (1,780)	11 hr	84.01 years
Neptune	4,500 (2,790)	16 hr	164.8 years
Pluto	5,900 (3,660)	6 days 9 hr	247.7 years

MAIN IDEAS

The five planets farthest from the sun are called the outer planets. Except for Pluto, they are the larger planets in the solar system. The planets revolve and rotate at different speeds.

QUESTIONS

Write your answers on a sheet of paper.

1. Which planet is described in each phrase below?
    a. has five rings
    b. has 10 moons
    c. farthest from the sun
    d. has a giant red spot
    e. about the same size as Uranus

Use the chart on page 222 to answer questions 2 through 4.

2. Which planet rotates in almost the same amount of time as Earth?
3. Which planet revolves around the sun in the smallest amount of time?
4. Which planet rotates in about half as much time as Earth?

SOMETHING EXTRA

Have you ever heard of NASA? Do you know what the letters in NASA stand for?

NASA is the National Aeronautics and Space Administration. Established in 1958, NASA is a government agency responsible for space research and travel programs.

Over 12,000 scientists, engineers, and technicians work for NASA. Some work at the headquarters in Washington, D.C. Others work at the John F. Kennedy Space Center at Cape Canaveral, the Lyndon Baines Johnson Space Center in Houston, or at many research centers throughout the country.

NASA scientists study photographs and rock samples from the moon, develop spacecrafts and equipment needed for space travel, and plan future space flights.

3 THE SUN

"Breaker, breaker. This is Leadfoot Larry about 40 km (25 mi) east of Cheyenne on Route 80. Can any of you good buddies tell me what is causing all this traffic? Over." Leadfoot Larry could hardly hear the answer about a truck accident. The message was lost in a crackling sound on the radio. Have you ever heard crackling sounds on a radio? What do you think might cause these sounds?

When you finish this lesson, you should be able to:

○ Describe some characteristics of the sun.

○ Explain one way in which the sun's energy can be used.

Star: An object in space that is made of hot gases.

The sun is a **star**. *Stars* are objects in space made of hot gases. The gases are so hot that they glow, giving off light. Therefore, unlike planets, stars give off their own light.

Life on Earth depends on the sun. Without the sun Earth would be an empty, cold place. There wouldn't be any plants or animals. The sun is Earth's main source of heat and light. At night, when the sun is not shining on some parts of Earth, the sky is dark and the temperature drops in those places.

The sun is the brightest star in the daytime sky. It is about 150 million km (93 million mi) from Earth.

Look at the picture below. Do you see dark spots on the sun's surface? These dark spots are called **sunspots**. *Sunspots* are places on the sun where the gases have cooled. Because the gases are cooler, they do not give off as much light as hot gases.

Sunspots: Dark spots on the sun.

Sometimes the sun's atmosphere has bright areas from which hot gases shoot out into space. These bright areas are called **solar flares**. *Solar flares* seem to affect things on Earth. They can interfere with radio messages. Can you give one reason why Leadfoot Larry's radio might not work properly?

Solar flares: Bright areas in the sun's atmosphere from which hot gases shoot out.

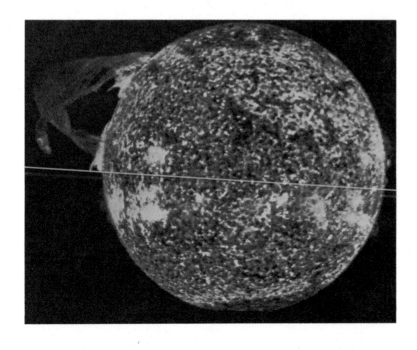

You have already learned about a solar eclipse. What
happens to the sun's light when a solar eclipse occurs?
Look at the picture below. It shows the sun during a solar eclipse. The moon is blocking most of the sun's light.
However, a faint white light can be seen around the
edges of the sun. This light is called the **corona** (co-**row**-
nah) of the sun. The word *corona* also means *crown*.
Why do you think the light is called the corona?

Look at the picture on the next page. It shows a house
that uses solar energy. The glass panels on the roof are
solar panels. Inside the solar panels are pipes carrying
water. The sun's light heats the water in the pipes. The
pipes carry the hot water to a storage tank under the
house. When hot water is needed to wash clothes, dishes,
or for bathing, the water is carried through other pipes
from the tank to the faucets. To heat the house, hot water
in pipes passes by a fan that blows air on the pipes. The
air is warmed by the hot water. The warm air is sent
around the house through air vents.

The sun is a star. The sun is 150 million km (93 million mi) away from Earth. The sun's sunspots, solar flares, and corona can be seen from Earth. Some people use solar energy to heat the air and water in their homes.

QUESTIONS

Write your answers on a sheet of paper.

1. Why does the sun give off light?
2. Describe each of the following:
    a. sunspots
    b. solar flares
    c. the corona
3. What is one way in which the sun's energy can be used?

CHAPTER  15

THE STARS AND BEYOND

1 STARS

The sun is the only star in our solar system. Yet, we can see thousands of stars in the night sky. The stars you see at night are much farther away from Earth than our sun. When you finish this lesson, you should be able to:

○ Tell how the distance of a star from Earth is measured.

○ Describe three ways in which stars differ from each other.

What units do you use to measure distance? You probably use kilometers (miles). However, the stars, except for the sun, are so far away that a kilometer (mile) is too small a unit to use. A star's distance from Earth is determined by how long it takes the star's light to reach Earth. The unit used is called a **light-year.** A *light-year* is the distance light travels in one year at the speed of light. The speed of light is 300,000 km/sec (186,000 mi/sec). The chart below lists the names of four stars. Next to each name is that star's distance from Earth. The light leaving the star Sirius (**sir**-ee-us) will take 8.8 years to travel to Earth. Which star listed is farthest from Earth? Which star is closest? Proxima Centauri (**prox**-eh-ma sen-**tor**-ee) is the closest star to Earth other than the sun.

Stars differ from each other in three ways: size, color, and brightness.

The smallest stars are a little larger than Earth. Small stars are called **dwarfs.** Stars that swell and become large are called **giants.** What do you think very large stars are called? **Supergiants,** of course!

Light-year: The distance light travels in one year.

Dwarfs: Small stars.

Giants: Stars that swell and become large.

Supergiants: Very large stars.

star	distance from Earth
Proxima Centauri	4.27 light–years
Sirius	8.8 light–years
Betelgeuse	587 light–years
Polaris	652 light–years

What color are the stars you have seen at night? You probably said white. Stars may be blue, white, yellow, orange, or red. Stars differ in color because of their different temperatures. Look at the flame shown. A hot gas is producing the flame. What colors do you see? The hottest part of the flame is at its bottom. What color is the bottom of the flame? If you said blue, you are right. The cooler part of the flame is orange.

Stars are balls of hot gases. Like the flame, stars with a high temperature are blue or blue-white in color. Red stars have low temperatures. Yellow and orange stars have medium temperatures. The chart below lists the names of some stars, their color, and their surface temperature. What color star is our sun?

star	color	temperature
Rigel	blue–white	12,000°C (21,632°F)
Sirius	white	10,500°C (18,932°F)
Sun	yellow	5,500°C (9,932°F)
Arcturus	orange	4,200°C (7,592°F)
Antares	red	3,000°C (5,432°F)

Magnitude: The brightness of a star as seen from Earth.

When you look at the stars at night, some stars look brighter than others. The brightness of a star as seen from Earth is called its **magnitude** (mag-nih-tood). A star's *magnitude* depends on its size, temperature, and distance from Earth. The brightest star in the night sky is Sirius although Proxima Centauri is the closest star to Earth. What star is the brightest in the daytime sky?

The distance of a star is indicated in light-years. Stars differ from each other in size, color, and magnitude.

QUESTIONS

Write your answers on a sheet of paper.

1. How is the speed of light used to indicate the distance of a star?
2. How do stars differ from each other in size?
3. Why are stars different colors?
4. What is meant by the magnitude of a star?

SOMETHING EXTRA

There are many satellites orbiting Earth. Only one is a moon. The others are human-made objects sent into orbit from Earth. These satellites contain instruments that give scientists a view of Earth they otherwise would not have.

One such satellite is called the *Landstat I*. It has special cameras that take pictures of Earth's surface. The pictures show patterns made on the surface by land, water, and plants. Places that might be good for fishing or planting are shown in these pictures. Places where oil may be found are also shown. Every place on the planet is scanned by the *Landstat I*.

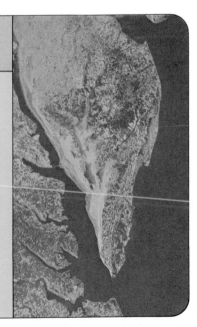

2 CONSTELLATIONS

What would you think if a friend told you there was a swan, a queen, a hunter, a little spoon, and a big spoon in the night sky? Many people believe that the stars form patterns in the sky that look like these things.

When you finish this lesson, you should be able to:

○ Tell the name given to groups of stars that form patterns in the sky.

○ Name and describe five of these groups of stars.

○ Explain why these groups of stars seem to move.

Constellations: Groups of stars that form patterns in the sky.

Groups of stars that form patterns in the sky are called **constellations** (kon-stel-**lay**-shuns). The patterns appear to look like animals, people, or objects. There are 88 *constellations*. You need a great deal of imagination to see some of them. Some are easy to see.

A. Cut out a square at one end of the shoebox. At the other end, cut out a circle so that the head of the flashlight fits into the hole.

B. Cut pieces of black paper and tracing paper that are slightly larger than the square opening.

C. On each sheet of tracing paper, trace one of the three groups of dots shown below.

D. Place each sheet of tracing paper over a piece of black paper.

E. Make a hole through each dot with an open safety pin so that the hole is made through the black paper too.

F. Tape one piece of black paper over the opening on the box.

G. Face that end of the box about 25 cm (10 in.) from a wall.

H. Darken the room. Turn on the flashlight.

   1. What do you see on the wall?

I. Repeat steps F, G, and H with the other pieces of black paper.

Materials
black construction
 paper
clear tape
flashlight
safety pin
scissor
shoebox
tracing paper

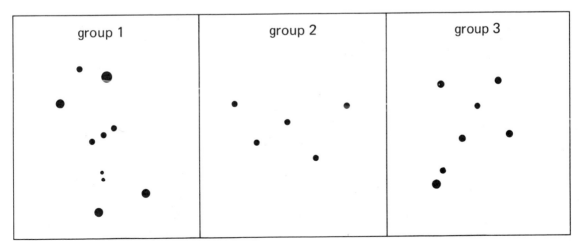

| group 1 | group 2 | group 3 |

Orion: A constellation.

The groups or patterns of dots that appeared on the wall are like patterns of stars seen in the sky. The first pattern is that of the constellation **Orion** (oh-**rye**-on). People think *Orion* looks like a hunter. The three stars across the center are supposed to be his belt. The small stars below his belt are his sword. The two stars above Orion's belt are his shoulders, and the two stars at the bottom of the constellation are the hunter's legs. The star at Orion's right shoulder is a red star named Betelgeuse (**bet**-tel-juz). The star at his left leg is a blue star named Rigel (**rye**-jel). Which star is hotter: Betelgeuse or Rigel?

Cassiopeia: A constellation.

The second pattern you saw is that of the constellation **Cassiopeia** (kass-ee-oh-**pee**-ah). People think the pattern forms the crown of the queen *Cassiopeia*. Look at the drawing of the queen. Do you see her crown?

Cygnus: A constellation.

The third pattern you saw is that of the constellation **Cygnus** (**sig**-nes). People think *Cygnus* looks like a swan. What do you think? There is a very bright star in Cygnus called Deneb (**den**-ebb). Deneb is a white star. Is it hotter or cooler than Rigel?

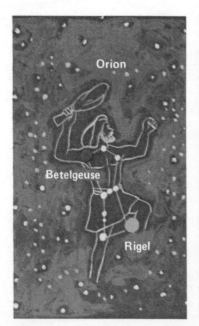

The constellations are not seen in the exact same place in the sky all night. They seem to move across the sky. The constellations seem to move because Earth is rotating.

The constellations seen from Earth in the winter are different from those seen in the summer. This occurs because Earth is in different places in space at different times of the year. However, there are two constellations that can be seen all year in the Northern Hemisphere. They are the **Big Dipper** and **Little Dipper**. No matter where in space Earth is, the North Pole of the planet is pointed toward these two constellations.

Big Dipper, Little Dipper: Constellations that are seen all year.

The *Big Dipper* and *Little Dipper* look like spoons or ladels. Look at the drawing below. The two stars at the end of the dipper of the Big Dipper are called pointer stars. An arrow drawn from these two stars will point to the last star of the handle of the Little Dipper. That star in the Little Dipper is called **Polaris** (pole-ar-ess), or the North Star. *Polaris* is a star that does not seem to move. It is always above Earth's North Pole.

Polaris: A star always above Earth's North Pole.

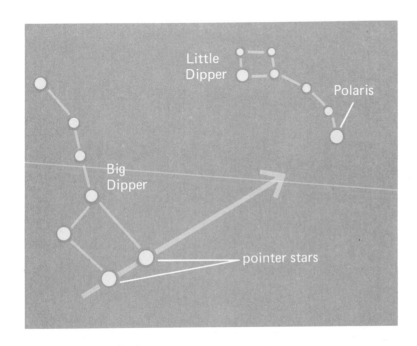

235

MAIN IDEAS

There are 88 constellations. People think the constellations look like people, animals, or objects. Orion, Cassiopeia, Cygnus, the Big Dipper, and the Little Dipper are constellations. Polaris is a star always seen above the North Pole.

QUESTIONS

Write your answers on a sheet of paper.

1. What name is given to groups of stars that form patterns in the sky?
2. Name and describe the three constellations below.
3. Which constellation includes Betelgeuse and Rigel?
4. What star is the last one in the handle of the Little Dipper?
5. Why do the constellations seem to move across the sky?
6. Why do we see different constellations at different times of the year?

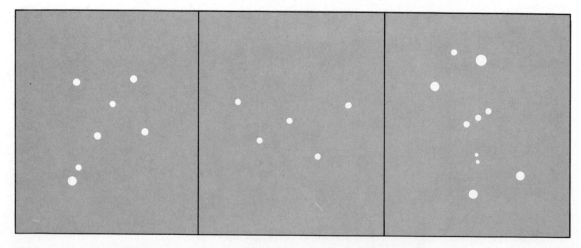

3 THE UNIVERSE

Imagine you are on a space platform whizzing through space. You are moving at about 1,000,000 km (620,000 mi) per hour. What do you think you would feel? What do you think you would see?

When you finish this lesson, you should be able to:

○ Name and describe the group of over 100 billion stars that includes our solar system.

○ Identify another large group of stars near Earth.

○ Describe three ideas about how everything in space was formed.

You are on a space platform. It is called Earth. As you travel through space you can see many stars and some planets. You are looking at part of a **galaxy** (gal-ax-ee).

Galaxy: A group of billions of stars.

237

A *galaxy* is a group of billions of stars. The galaxy Earth is in, called Our Galaxy or the Milky Way, contains about 100 billion stars and our solar system. Look at the drawings below. If viewed from the side, the Milky Way is shaped like a huge disc with a bulge at its center. From above, it appears to have arms that spiral around the center. That is why the Milky Way is called a spiral galaxy. The distance from one edge of the Milky Way to the other is about 100,000 light-years. The solar system is believed to be about 30,000 light-years from the center of the Milky Way. Look at the drawings again. The arrows point to the position of the sun in the solar system.

You are moving around the center of the Milky Way at 1,000,000 km (620,000 mi) per hour. At that speed it would take you about one second to travel from Philadelphia to Washington, D.C., or from Los Angeles to San Diego.

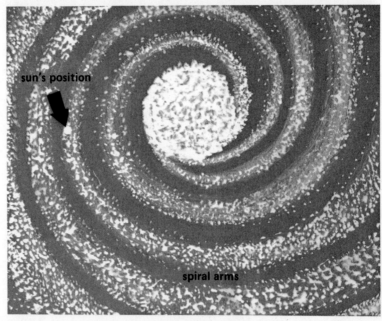

sun's position

spiral arms

The Milky Way is not the only galaxy. Millions of galaxies have been seen by scientists using special equipment. Sixteen of these galaxies are within 3 million light-years of ours. One of the closest is called the **Andromeda Galaxy** (an-**drom**-med-dah). The picture on the cover of this book is of the *Andromeda Galaxy*. The galaxy was named Andromeda because from Earth the galaxy is seen in the same area as a constellation named Andromeda. However, the galaxy is millions of light-years farther away from Earth than the constellation. The Andromeda Galaxy is also a spiral galaxy. How is a spiral galaxy shaped?

Andromeda Galaxy: One of the closest galaxies to Our Galaxy.

The Milky Way contains dust and gases. Sometimes the dust and gases form clouds. The clouds are called **nebulae** (**neb**-you-lye). Look at the two pictures below. The first picture is of the Orion *nebula*. The second is the Horse Head nebula. Do you see a horse's head?

Nebulae: Clouds of dust and gas.

Universe: All the galaxies and the space they exist in.

All of the galaxies and the space they exist in is called the **universe** (**you**-nih-vers). Scientists have wondered how the *universe* was formed. There is no definite explanation. However, there are many theories about how the universe was formed. A theory is a possible explanation for what is observed.

One theory states that over 10 billion years ago everything in the universe was packed together. Then a giant explosion occurred. Everything went flying outward into space, forming planets, stars, and galaxies.

Another theory states that galaxies are constantly moving out of the universe. New galaxies are formed to take their place.

A third theory states that the universe explodes, comes together, and explodes again. This is thought to occur about every eighty billion years.

MAIN IDEAS

The Milky Way contains about 100 billion stars and our solar system. The Milky Way and the Andromeda Galaxy are spiral galaxies. Clouds of gas and dust in the Milky Way are called nebulae. There are many theories about how the universe was formed

QUESTIONS

Write your answers on a sheet of paper.

1. What name is given to the group of 100 billion stars that includes our solar system?
2. Describe the shape of the Milky Way.
3. What galaxy is one of the closest to the Milky Way? How did that galaxy get its name?
4. Name and describe three theories about how the universe was formed.

 16 STUDYING THE UNIVERSE

1 TOOLS USED TO STUDY SPACE

In this unit you have learned many things about distant objects. How is it possible for scientists to see and study objects so far away?

When you finish this lesson, you should be able to:

○ Tell the name given to scientists who study objects in space.

○ Name and describe instruments scientists use to study distant objects.

Astronomers: Scientists who study objects in space.

Telescope: An instrument used to study distant objects.

Refracting telescope: A telescope in which light is bent.

Convex lens: A piece of glass thicker in the middle than at the edges.

Scientists who study objects in space are called **astronomers** (a-**stron**-oh-mers). Galileo was a famous *astronomer*. He was the first person to look closely at the moon through a **telescope** (**tell**-eh-scope). A *telescope* is an instrument that makes distant objects appear closer and larger.

Astronomers use three types of telescopes. One type is the **refracting telescope** (ree-**frak**-ting). The word *refract* means *to bend*. In a *refracting telescope,* the light from the distant object is bent. How is light bent?

Light can be bent if it passes through a piece of glass thicker in the middle than at the edges. A piece of glass shaped this way is called a **convex lens**. A refracting telescope is a long tube with a *convex lens* at each end. Look at the diagram below after you read about how a refracting telescope works.

Light from a distant object enters the wider end of the telescope. The light passes through a large convex lens. The light is bent and a small image or picture of the distant object appears. A smaller convex lens at the narrow end of the telescope enlarges the image. To the person looking into the telescope at the narrow end, the distant object appears large and close.

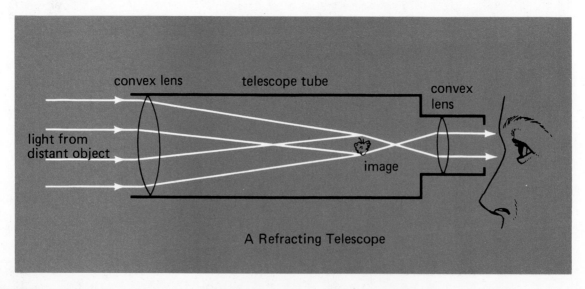

A Refracting Telescope

Another type of telescope is the **reflecting telescope** (re-**flek**-ting). The word *reflect* means *to bounce off*. In a *reflecting telescope*, the light from the distant object is reflected.

Look at the diagram below after you read about how a reflecting telescope works. Light from a distant object enters the open end of the telescope. The light travels through the tube to a mirror that is curved inward. It is called a **concave mirror**. The light is reflected from the *concave mirror* and an image of the distant object appears at a flat mirror. The flat mirror directs the image sideways to a convex lens. The convex lens enlarges the image. To the person looking into the telescope, the distant object appears large and close.

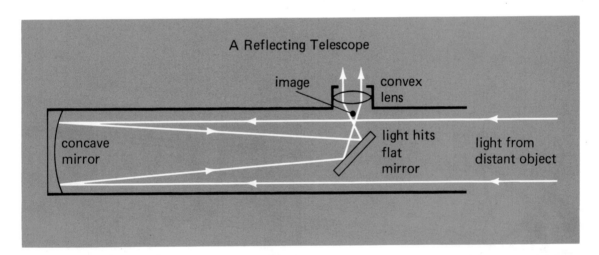

A Reflecting Telescope

image — convex lens — light hits flat mirror — light from distant object — concave mirror

The largest reflecting telescope is on Mount Palomar in California. It is called the Hale telescope. The concave mirror in the Hale telescope is about 5 m (16⅔ ft) wide. The picture on the left shows the Hale telescope.

The largest refracting telescope is at the Yerkes Observatory in Wisconsin. Its lens is about 1 m (3½ ft) wide. Refracting telescopes cannot have very large lenses because the center of the lenses would sag. A concave mirror in a reflecting telescope can be very large because the mirror can be supported from the back.

A third type of telescope is the radio telescope. A radio telescope is shaped like a soup bowl. In its center is an antenna. The antenna is pointed toward the sky. Astronomers do not see distant objects with this type of telescope. Instead, the radio telescope records sounds made by objects in space. Astronomers have found that the sun, some planets, distant galaxies, and the stars give off radio waves. The radio waves travel through space and are picked up by the antenna. The antenna passes the waves to a receiver. The receiver changes the waves into a pattern, which is drawn on a roll of paper in the recorder. The pattern tells astronomers the position of the object. One of the largest radio telescopes is at Arecibo, Puerto Rico.

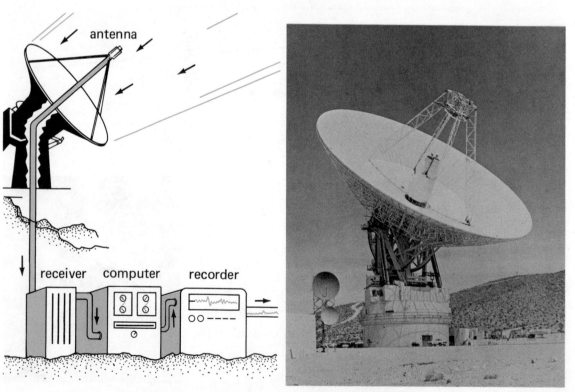

Astronomers use three types of telescopes to learn about distant objects. In a reflecting telescope light from a distant object is reflected. In a refracting telescope light from a distant object is refracted. A radio telescope records radio waves given off by distant objects.

QUESTIONS

Write your answers on a sheet of paper.

1. What is the name given to scientists who study object in space?
2. Name three types of telescopes.
3. Describe how refracting and reflecting telescopes enlarge distant objects.
4. What do scientists learn from a radio telescope?

SOMETHING EXTRA

A long time ago scientists thought Earth was at the center of the solar system. However, they were incorrect. What is at the center of the solar system?

A German astronomer, Johannes Kepler, was one of the first scientists to explain the motion of the planets around the sun. He believed that every planet followed an oval-shaped path around the sun. He called the time in which a planet makes one trip around the sun a period. What do we call this amount of time? Kepler also experimented with lenses and how they could be used to magnify distant objects.

Kepler's family was very poor. They could not pay for his education. But Kepler's interest in learning made it possible for him to earn many scholarships from schools he wished to attend.

2 HUMANS IN SPACE

"Houston . . . the *Eagle* has landed." Do you know who said those historic words on July 20, 1969? Where do you think those words were spoken?

When you finish this lesson, you should be able to:

○ Tell the names of some people who have traveled in space.

○ Tell what space travelers do on the moon.

In 1957 the Soviet Union sent the first spacecraft, named *Sputnik I*, into orbit around Earth. Why was *Sputnik I* called a satellite? One year later, the United States sent a spacecraft, named *Explorer I*, into space. These two events marked the beginning of space exploration through space travel.

One of the first passengers to travel in a spacecraft was Little Joe 3, an American monkey. Scientists wanted to study the effects of space travel on animals before sending humans. Americans who travel in space are called **astronauts** (a-stro-nots). Russian space travelers are called **cosmonauts** (koz-mow-nots). The first person in space was a *cosmonaut* named Yuri Gagarin (**your**-ree ga-**gar**-in). In a spacecraft, he made one orbit around Earth on April 12, 1961. The flight took one hour and 48 minutes. An *astronaut* named John Glenn was the first American to orbit Earth. His spacecraft was named *Friendship 7*.

In the 1960's the United States and Soviet Union sent many spacecrafts into space. Some had passengers. Others did not. In 1963 Valentina Tereshkova (**val**-en-tee-nah tear-ish-**koh**-vah), a Russian cosmonaut, was the first woman in space.

Look at the picture. What do you think the astronaut is doing? The astronaut is Edward White. He was the first human to walk in space. What do you see behind him?

Astronauts: Americans who travel in space.

Cosmonauts: Russians who travel in space.

The words at the beginning of this lesson were spoken by Michael Collins. He was speaking to people at the United States Space Control Center in Houston. Collins was speaking from a spacecraft that was orbiting the moon. The *Eagle* he mentioned was not a bird. It was the first spacecraft with passengers to land on the moon's surface. Neil Armstrong and Edward Aldrin were in the *Eagle*. Neil Armstrong was the first human to step on the moon's surface.

Retroreflector: A piece of equipment used by astronauts.

The astronauts left some equipment on the moon such as a **retroreflector** (ret-tro-ree-**flek**-tore). In this activity you will make a *retroreflector*.

Materials
black construction
  paper
clear tape
flashlight
pencil
2 small mirrors

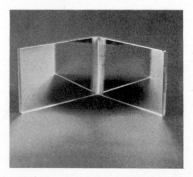

A. Tape the two small mirrors together as shown in the picture.

B. With a pencil make a hole through the center of the black paper.

C. Cover the flashlight with the black paper so that the hole is directly in front of the bulb.

D. Place the mirrors anywhere in the room. Turn off the lights.

E. Hold the flashlight beside your eye and shine the light at the mirrors.

   1. What do you see in the mirrors?

F. Move the flashlight away from your head by stretching your arm outward from your side.

   2. What happened to the light in the mirrors?

The retroreflectors on the moon are like the mirrors you used. Scientists shine light from Earth to the retroreflectors. The light is reflected back to Earth. The scientists measure the time it takes the light to travel from Earth to the retroreflector and back to Earth again. Then they know how far away the retroreflector is from Earth. Scientists use retroreflectors to measure changes in the distance of the moon from Earth.

Astronauts have made many trips to the moon. While on the moon they took thousands of pictures. They collected rocks to bring back to Earth for scientists to study. The astronauts traveled long distances over the surface of the moon.

MAIN IDEAS

The United States and Soviet Union have sent many spacecrafts into space. The first American to orbit Earth was John Glenn. The first woman in space was the cosmonaut Valentina Tereshkova. Humans have traveled to and landed on the moon.

QUESTIONS

Write your answers on a sheet of paper.

1. Who was the first human to travel in space? walk in space? stand on the moon?
2. How are astronauts and cosmonauts different?
3. What do astronauts do on the moon?

UNIT SUMMARY

Earth rotates and revolves in space. Earth's rotation causes daytime and nighttime. The tilt of Earth causes seasons.

The moon is a satellite of Earth. The moon's surface has craters, mountains, and marias. The shapes of the moon are called phases. When the moon passes between Earth and the sun, a solar eclipse occurs. When the Earth passes between the moon and sun, a lunar eclipse occurs.

Our solar system contains nine planets, their moons, and the sun. Mercury, Venus, Earth, and Mars are called the inner planets. Jupiter, Saturn, Uranus, Neptune, and Pluto are called the outer planets. Planets do not give off their own light.

Our sun is a star. Stars give off their own light. Stars differ from each other in size, color, and magnitude. Groups of stars form patterns in the sky called constellations.

The Milky Way, a galaxy, is a group of billions of stars. It includes a solar system. Ours is not the only galaxy. All of the galaxies and the space they exist in is called the universe.

Astronomers use telescopes to study distant objects. They use refracting, reflecting, and radio telescopes. Some distances in space are measured in light-years.

CHECK YOURSELF

1. Why do places on Earth have a daytime, nighttime, and seasons?
2. What is a satellite? What satellite of Earth has craters, mountains, and marias?
3. Why does the moon have phases?
4. What is the position of the moon, sun, and Earth during a solar eclipse? a lunar eclipse?

5. Name the planets in the solar system. Briefly describe each planet.
6. What are sunspots? solar flares? the sun's corona?
7. What star, other than the sun, is the closest to Earth?
8. Name three ways in which stars differ from each other.
9. What star is the brightest star in our night sky?
10. What are constellations? Name three.
11. Why is Polaris also called the North Star?
12. What is the Milky Way? What shape is the Milky Way? Name another galaxy that is the same shape.
13. Name and describe three types of telescopes.

PROJECTS

1. People say that if you wish on a shooting star your wish will come true. Find out about shooting stars. Library books about objects in space will be helpful. Are shooting stars really stars? What do you think about wishing on a star?
2. Build a model spacecraft. You can use boxes, cups, plastic containers, fabrics, wire, crayons, aluminum foil, and many other materials to make your model. When it is completed, show your model to the class.
3. Look for the moon every night for the next 30 nights. Draw the phase you may observe each night and write the date on which you see it next to the drawing. What phases did you observe? How many times did you see each phase? Find out how the phases of the moon were used to make calendars. Library and reference books will be helpful.
4. Scientists are able to predict when lunar eclipses will occur. The following dates are when total eclipses will occur: July 17, 1981, July 6, 1982, December 30, 1982, and June 25, 1983. Perhaps you will be able to observe some of them.

Scientists did not invent electricity; they discovered it. There are written records that electricity was observed and explored more than 2,500 years ago. However, electricity has only been put to use in the past 100 years. Think of the many ways you use electricity in your daily life.

Knowledge about magnetism was put to use much sooner than electricity. The compass, which contains a magnet, is thought to have been developed in ancient China.

This unit is about electricity and magnetism: what they are, how they are used, and how they are related to each other.

6 ELECTRICITY AND MAGNETISM

CHAPTER 17 ELECTRICITY

1 STATIC ELECTRICITY

Walk across a carpet on a cool, dry day. Then touch a metal doorknob. What do you think will happen? Do you know why?

When you finish this lesson, you should be able to:

○ Describe an electrical property of all matter.

○ Tell why objects sometimes move away from or toward each other.

○ Tell the name of a type of electricity.

A. Tear the sheet of paper into small pieces.

B. Rub the comb back and forth quickly with the wool.

C. Hold the comb about 2.5 cm (1 in.) above the pieces of paper.

    1. What happened to the paper?

Materials
comb
paper
wool, 15 cm (6 in.)
  square

    In this activity you rubbed the comb with the wool. Then the comb attracted the small bits of paper. Why do you think the comb attracted the paper?

    All matter, including the comb, wool, and paper, contains tiny electrical particles. The electrical property of each particle is called its **charge (charj)**. Some particles have a positive electric *charge*. Others have a negative electric charge. However, we can rub or pull negative charges off one object and place them on another. When an object gains or loses negative charges the object is said to be electrically charged.

Charge: The electrical property of particles of matter.

255

All matter has an equal number of positive and negative charges. An object that loses negative charges is left with a greater number of positive charges. That object is said to be positively charged. An object that gains negative charges is said to be negatively charged.

Look at the first picture above. Both balloons have been negatively charged. When two negatively charged objects are brought close to each other they will **repel** (ree-**pell**), or move away from, each other. The same thing happens when two positively charged objects are brought close together. The balloons move away from each other because the same or like charges *repel* each other.

Look at the second picture. One balloon has been positively charged. The other has been negatively charged. What happens when two oppositely charged objects are brought close together? The balloons move toward each other because unlike charges attract each other.

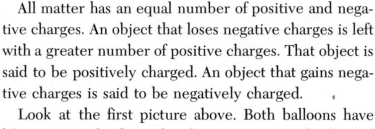

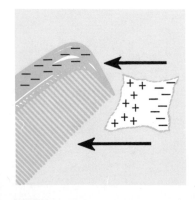

When you rubbed the comb with the wool, negative charges were rubbed off the wool onto the comb. The negatively charged comb was brought near the papers. The negative charges in each paper were then repelled to the side of the paper away from the comb. This made the side of the paper closest to the comb positively charged. The positively charged side of the paper was then attracted to the negatively charged comb.

The type of electricity produced in an object that gains or loses negative charges is called **static electricity**. Objects with *static electricity* may attract or repel each other. They may also attract objects that do not have static electricity.

When you walk across a carpet, negative charges are rubbed off the rug onto your body. You become negatively charged. The extra negative charges in your body are attracted to the positive charges in the doorknob. The negative charges leaving your body cause an electric shock.

Static electricity: A type of electricity produced when objects gain or lose negative charges.

MAIN IDEAS

All matter contains negative and positive charges. Like charges repel each other. Unlike charges attract each other. Objects can gain or lose negative charges. An object that gains or loses negative charges has static electricity.

QUESTIONS

Write your answers on a sheet of paper.

1. When is an object said to be electrically charged?
2. Does a negatively charged object have more negative or more positive charges?
3. How can negative charges be taken off one object and placed on another?
4. Tell what happens when a negatively charged object is brought close to each of the following:
   a. a positively charged object
   b. a negatively charged object
5. What type of electricity is produced when an object gains or loses negative charges?

2 CURRENT ELECTRICITY

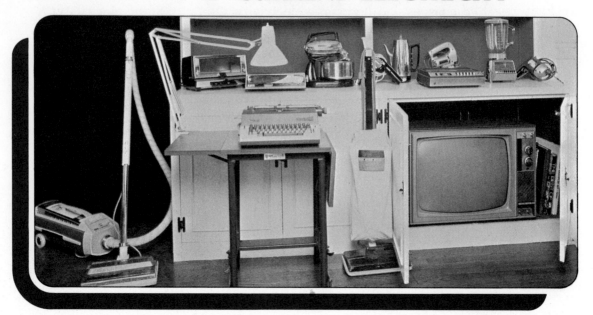

The kind of electricity you are most familiar with is used by the appliances shown above. It is not static electricity. The word *static* means *not moving*. The kind of electricity used by toasters, televisions, and radios is electricity that occurs when charges move. When you finish this lesson, you should be able to:

○ Tell the name of the type of electricity produced when charges move.

○ Describe the path through which charges can move.

○ Describe materials that do and do not allow electricity to flow through them easily.

Current electricity: A flow of negative charges.

Circuit: The path through which negative charges flow.

When electric charges move from one place to another, **current electricity** is produced. *Current electricity* is a flow of negative charges. The negative charges need a path through which they can flow or move. The path through which negative charges flow is called a **circuit** (sir-kett).

Look at the first picture below. It shows a *circuit*. There are four parts to the circuit shown. There is a source of electric charges (dry cell), a path through which the charges flow (wires), a user of the electricity (lightbulb), and a switch. In a circuit, the current flows from the source, through the wires, switch, and user of the electricity, and then returns to the source.

When all the parts of the circuit are connected so that the current can flow, the circuit is said to be closed. When any part of the circuit is not connected, the current cannot flow. The circuit is said to be open. The switch in a circuit is often used to open or close the circuit. The circuit is open when the switch is up. When do you think the circuit is closed?

Some materials allow current to flow through them easily. These materials are called **conductors** (con-**duk**-terz). Materials that do not allow current to flow through them easily, if at all, are called **insulators** (in-sue-lay-terz). On the next page is an activity in which you will find out if a material is a *conductor* or *insulator*.

Conductors: Materials that allow current to flow through them easily.

Insulators: Materials that do not allow current to flow through them easily.

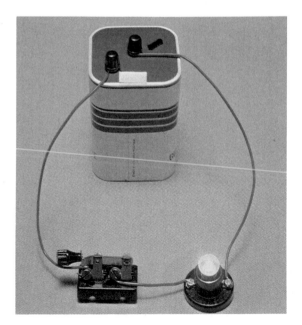
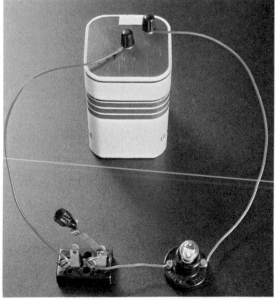

ACTIVITY

Materials
aluminum foil
door key
dry cell, 1.5 volts
lightbulb with socket
paper
pencil
2 pieces of wire,
  30 cm (12 in.) long
rubber band
screwdriver

A. Make a chart like the one shown.

B. Connect the wire, lightbulb, and dry cell as shown in the picture.

C. Hold the covered part of the wire. Touch the uncovered end of each wire to the aluminum foil.

1. What happened to the lightbulb?

D. On your chart, indicate if the aluminum foil is a conductor or an insulator by writing a check mark.

E. Repeat steps C and D for each item on your list.

item tested	conductor	insulator
aluminum foil		
door key		
paper		
nickel		
rubber band		

Paper and a rubber band do not allow current to flow through them. They are insulators. Wood, glass, and cloth are examples of other insulators. Aluminum foil, a key, and a nickel allow current to flow through them. They are conductors. They are also made of metals. Most metals are good conductors of electric current.

Current electricity is a flow of negative charges. A circuit is a path through which negative charges can flow. Conductors allow current to flow through them easily. Insulators do not allow current to flow through them easily, if at all.

QUESTIONS

Write your answers on a sheet of paper.

1. What type of electricity is produced by a flow of negative charges?
2. What word describes the path through which negative charges flow?
3. List four parts of a circuit.
4. How are open and closed circuits different from each other?
5. What is a conductor? an insulator?

SOMETHING EXTRA

Too often people try to repair their own electrical appliances. This can be very dangerous unless the person has a knowledge of electricity and wiring.

People who are trained to repair small appliances or large generators are **electricians** (ee-lek-**trish**-unz). *Electricians* also install, maintain, and inspect electrical systems. They learn their skills in several ways. Some attend trade schools. Others learn by working with experienced electricians or are trained in the armed forces. Many states require that electricians obtain licenses by passing an exam that tests their knowledge of electricity.

3 A KIND OF CIRCUIT

Everyone was excited about decorating the Christmas tree this year. Barbara had placed the lightbulbs in the sockets. Ed was hanging the tinsel. Finally, the tree was decorated. The switch for the lights was closed but the lights did not go on. Barbara looked over all the lightbulbs. She found that one was loose in its socket. After tightening that bulb all the lights went on.

When you finish this lesson, you should be able to:

○ Tell the name of and describe a type of circuit in which there is only one path for the charges to flow.

○ Draw a circuit diagram.

The lights on a Christmas tree are part of a circuit. The lights are the users of the electric current. The lights on Barbara's and Ed's tree are connected one after another. The type of circuit in which the parts are connected one after another is called a **series circuit.** In a *series circuit* there is only one path through which the charges can flow. The charges flow from the source through the wire and each bulb, and back to the source. If the circuit has a switch, the current flows through the switch too.

Series circuit: A circuit with only one path through which the charges can flow.

A. Connect a series circuit as shown below. Then close the switch.

   1. What happened to the lightbulbs?

B. Unscrew one lightbulb.

   2. What happened to the other lightbulb?

Materials
dry cell, 1.5 volts
2 lightbulbs in sockets
screwdriver
switch
4 pieces of wire, 30
   cm (12 in.) long

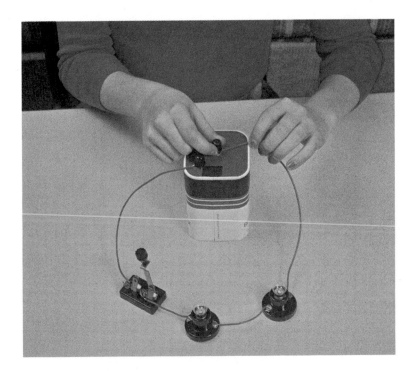

The lights on some Christmas trees are connected in a series circuit. Barbara and Ed found out that if one lightbulb did not work, none of the lightbulbs would light. The same thing happened in the activity. When you unscrewed one lightbulb, the other one went off. If one light goes off in a series circuit, the circuit is broken and all the lights go off. The charges cannot continue to flow through the whole circuit.

Look at the pictures below. Both show a series circuit. How are the circuits different from each other?

The amount of current flowing through both circuits is the same. However, when more lightbulbs are added to a series circuit, the light from each lightbulb is dimmer. In a series circuit, the users of the current must share the available current.

Scientists often draw diagrams of a circuit. They use symbols to represent the parts of the circuit. These symbols are shown on the chart on the next page. When scientists draw circuit diagrams, the diagram is usually drawn in a rectangular or box shape.

Look at the diagram below. It shows a series circuit. How many lightbulbs are in the circuit? Is the switch open or closed? Can you point to the dry cell and wires?

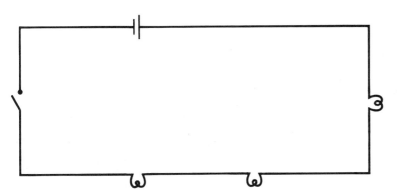

circuit part		symbol
dry cell	▯	‖
lightbulb	🔆	m
open switch	◢	⌐•‒
closed switch	◢	———
wire	∿	———

MAIN IDEAS

In a series circuit there is only one path through which the charges can flow. The parts of the circuit are connected in a series. The circuit is broken if one lightbulb or user of the electricity does not work. Scientists draw diagrams of circuits.

QUESTIONS

Write your answers on a sheet of paper.

1. In what type of circuit is there only one path through which the charges can flow?
2. In a series circuit, what happens to all the lightbulbs in the circuit if one lightbulb goes off?
3. Which lightbulbs in a series circuit with the same amount of current would appear brighter: three lightbulbs or six lightbulbs?
4. Draw a diagram of a circuit that has one dry cell, wires, three lightbulbs, and a closed switch.

4 MORE ABOUT CIRCUITS

The person in the picture above is reading under a lamp. How many lightbulbs does the lamp have? How many lightbulbs are lit? Do you think the lightbulbs are connected in a series circuit?

When you finish this lesson, you should be able to:

○ Name and describe a type of circuit in which there is more than one path through which the charges can flow.

○ Explain why house circuits are this type of circuit.

Parallel circuit: A circuit with more than one path through which the charges can flow.

The lightbulbs in the lamp shown in the picture above are not connected in series. One lightbulb is not lit but the other two are lit. These lightbulbs are part of a type of circuit called a **parallel circuit**. In a *parallel circuit* there is more than one path through which the charges can flow.

A. Connect a parallel circuit as shown below.

B. Close the switch.

    1. What happened to the lightbulbs?

C. Unscrew one lightbulb.

2. What happened to the other lightbulbs?

D. As you unscrew another lightbulb, look at the remaining lit bulb.

    3. Did the light from the lightbulb get brighter or dimmer?

Materials
dry cell, 1.5 volts
3 lightbulbs in sockets
7 pieces of wire,
 30 cm (12 in.) long
screwdriver
switch

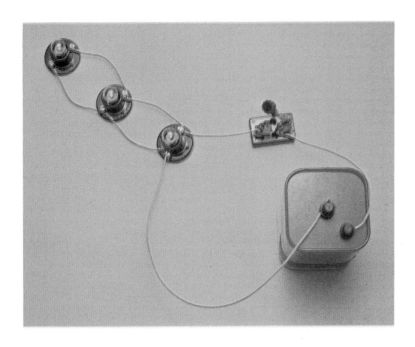

In a parallel circuit each lightbulb or user of the electricity is on its own path. Therefore, if one lightbulb goes off, the others will stay lit. The current flowing through each lightbult is separate from the current flowing through the others. Because of this, adding or taking away lightbulbs does not change the brightness of the lightbulbs.

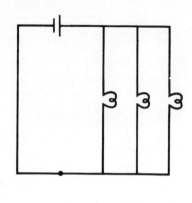

The diagram shown here is of a parallel circuit. How many lightbulbs are in this circuit? If all the lightbulbs are the same, will any one lightbulb be brighter than another? In this circuit, how many paths can the charges flow through?

Think about the lights and appliances in your home. If you turn off the lights in the kitchen, will the lights in the living room stay on? Can you play a radio even if the lights in the room are off?

All house circuits are parallel circuits. This allows you to turn lights and appliances on and off without affecting other users of electricity.

MAIN IDEAS

In a parallel circuit there is more than one path through which the charges can flow. Each user of the electricity is on its own path. All house circuits are parallel circuits.

QUESTIONS

Write your answers on a sheet of paper.

1. In what type of circuit is there more than one path through which the charges can flow?
2. In a parallel circuit, what happens to the lightbulbs in the circuit if half of them go off?
3. How does adding lightbulbs to a parallel circuit affect the brightness of the lightbulbs?
4. Why is it necessary for house circuits to be parallel circuits?

CHAPTER  18 MAGNETISM

1 MAGNETS

The picture above shows a huge object that was used to pick up nails and metal pieces. Can you identify the place where it was used? After an official ceremony in front of the White House, this huge object helped collect some of the debris left there.

When you finish this lesson, you should be able to:

○ Name and describe an object that picks up or attracts iron, nickel, and cobalt.

○ Tell the word that describes the space around this object.

Magnets: Objects that pick up or attract iron, nickel, or cobalt.

Poles: The ends of a magnet.

Magnets are objects that pick up or attract iron, nickel, or cobalt. A *magnet* will not pick up or attract materials such as paper, wood, plastic, tin, or rubber.

The ends of a magnet are called the **poles**. Magnets are strongest at their *poles*. Magnets have two poles: a north pole and a south pole. The letters *S* and *N* on the ends of a magnet indicate which is the north and which is the south pole.

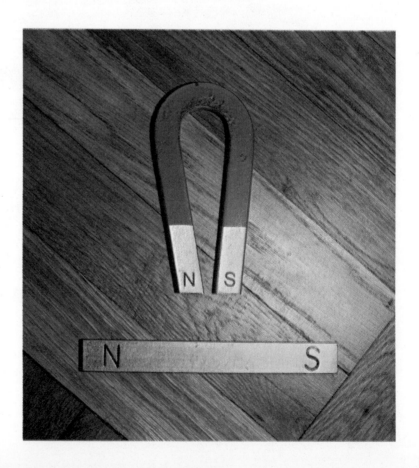

A. Place one magnet on your desk. Place the plastic sheet over the magnet.

B. Sprinkle the iron filings onto the plastic sheet as shown below.

C. Gently tap the edge of the plastic sheet until the iron filings form a pattern.

1. How would you describe the pattern formed by the iron filings?

Materials
bar magnet
iron filings
plastic sheet, 15 cm
(6 in.) square

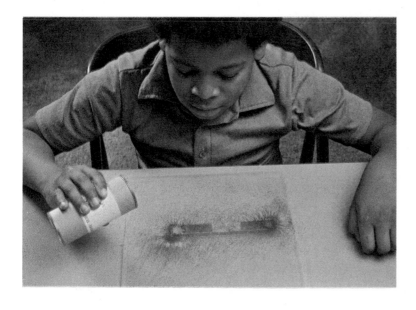

The iron filings formed a pattern of lines like that shown in the picture at the top of the next page. Lines that form around a magnet in this way are called **lines of force**. *Lines of force* show that the space around a magnet has a magnetic force. The space around a magnet in which there is a magnetic force is called a **magnetic field**. The lines of force show where the *magnetic field* is located. At what part of the magnet are the lines of force closer together? Why do you think the lines of force are closer together at the poles?

Lines of force: Lines around a magnet that show where the magnetic force is found.

Magnetic field: The space around a magnet in which there is a magnetic force.

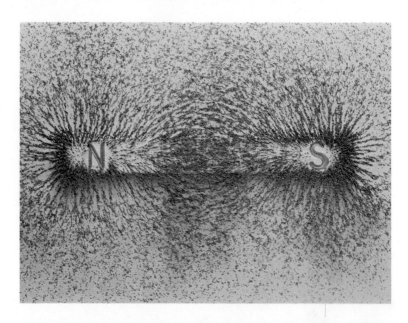

Look at the two pictures below. The first picture shows the lines of force around two magnets. The N pole of one magnet and the S pole of the other magnet have been brought close to each other. In the second picture the N poles of both magnets have been brought close to each other. How are the lines of force shown in both pictures different from each other?

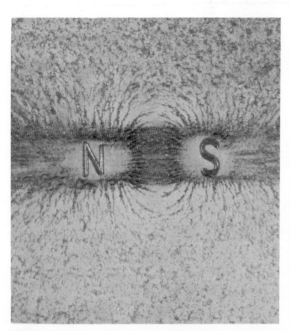

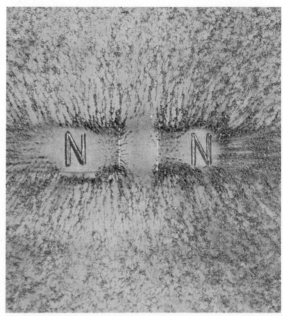

In the bottom left picture on page 272 the lines of force show a magnetic force from the N pole of one magnet to the S pole of the other. This means that the poles of the magnets are attracting each other. N and S poles are opposite poles. Opposite magnetic poles attract each other.

In the bottom right picture on page 272 the lines of the force do not show an attracting magnetic force between the two poles. The lines of force show that the magnetic force goes away from the poles. This means that the poles of the magnets are repelling each other. Two N poles are the same, or like, poles. Like magnetic poles repel each other. Do you think two S poles will attract or repel each other?

MAIN IDEAS

Magnets attract iron, nickel, and cobalt. Magnets are strongest at their poles. Opposite magnetic poles attract each other. Like magnetic poles repel each other.

QUESTIONS

Write your answers on a sheet of paper.

1. What object picks up or attracts iron, nickel, and cobalt?
2. What parts of a magnet are strongest?
3. What words describe the space around a magnet?
4. Why are the lines of force around two opposite magnetic poles different from the lines of force around two like magnetic poles?

2 A SPECIAL KIND OF MAGNET

In 1819, a Danish scientist named Hans Christian Oersted wanted to find out if magnetism and electricity were related. Oersted placed a compass needle near the wire in a circuit. A compass needle is a small magnet. When an electric current moved through the wire in Oersted's circuit, the pole of the compass needle changed direction. What do you think made the compass needle change direction?

When you finish this lesson, you should be able to:

○ Tell why and how current electricity can be used to make a kind of magnet.

○ List three ways in which the strength of this kind of magnet can be increased.

Oersted believed that there must be a magnetic force around a wire through which current electricity is flowing. Look at the picture below. A card was placed around the wire in the circuit shown. Iron filings were sprinkled on the card. The iron filings formed lines of force around the wire. The lines of force formed a circular pattern.

The lines of force show that there is a magnetic force in the space around a wire through which current is flowing. Therefore, current electricity is surrounded by a magnetic field. How can we put this discovery to use?

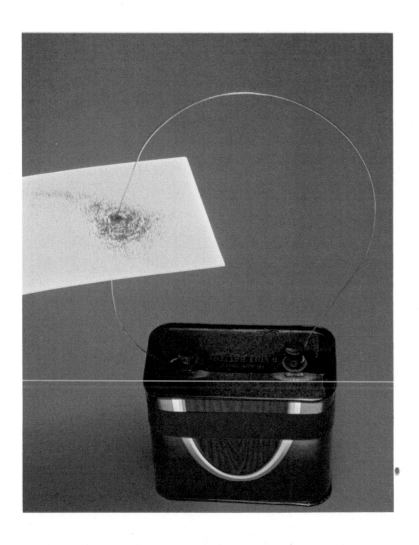

ACTIVITY

Materials
dry cell, 1.5 volts
iron nail
paper clips
screwdriver
switch
1 piece of wire, 30 cm
  (12 in.) long
1 piece of wire, 60 cm
  (24 in.) long

A. Attach the short wire from the dry cell to one side of the switch. Attach the long wire from the other side of the switch. Make sure the switch is open.

B. Wrap the long wire around the iron nail, as shown in the picture, at least 20 times. Attach the end of the wire to the dry cell.

C. Place the clips on your desk.

D. Close the switch. Try to pick up the paper clips with the nail.

  1. What happened?

E. Open the switch.
  2. What happened to the paper clips?

In the activity you used electricity to make a magnet. When electric current flowed through the wire wrapped around the iron nail, the nail picked up the paper clips. When you opened the switch, the current could not flow and the paper clips fell off the nail.

The type of magnet you made is an **electromagnet** (ee-lek-tro-**mag**-net). An *electromagnet* is made with current electricity and will attract iron, nickel, and cobalt. The paper clips are made of steel. Steel is made from iron.

The picture below shows a large electromagnet. It has a huge piece of iron that becomes an electromagnet when the person in the cab connects the circuit. This electromagnet is very strong and can pick up heavy objects.

Electromagnet: A magnet made with current electricity.

There are three ways to increase the strength of an electromagnet. Look at the pictures below. The first picture shows an electromagnet that has one dry cell and one iron nail wrapped with wire 15 times. How many paper clips does the electromagnet attract? Look at the next three pictures. How has the electromagnet been changed?

The strength of an electromagnet can be increased by adding more current to the circuit. How was this done in the second circuit shown? In the third picture, adding another iron nail increased the strength of an electromagnet. The last picture shows how the strength of an electromagnet can be increased by wrapping the wire around the iron nail many more times.

Current electricity can be used to make a magnet. The type of magnet made is called an electromagnet. There are three ways in which the strength of an electromagnet can be increased.

QUESTIONS

Write your answers on a sheet of paper.

1. Why can current electricity be used to make a magnet?
2. Tell how an electromagnet can be made.
3. List three ways in which the strength of an electromagnet can be increased.

SOMETHING EXTRA

Before the invention of the telegraph there was no way to send messages quickly over long distances. In 1844, Samuel Morse invented a device that could send messages quickly. The device contained an electromagnet and was called a telegraph. The first telegraph message was sent from Washington, D.C., to Baltimore, Maryland.

A telegraph message is sent as a series of clicks. Two clicks close together are called a *dot*. Two clicks further apart are called a *dash*. Dots and dashes represent letters in the alphabet. For example, three dots and a dash is the letter *V*. One dash and one dot is the letter *N*. The dots, dashes, and letters they represent are called the Morse Code. Telegraph operators know how to translate a written message to be sent to Morse Code and Morse Code to a written message.

3 MOVING MAGNETS

In the last lesson you learned that current electricity can produce magnetism. Can magnetism produce current electricity? In 1831, an English scientist named Michael Faraday did an experiment to find out.

When you finish this lesson, you should be able to:

○ Tell how magnetism produces current electricity.

○ Describe a machine in which magnetism produces current electricity.

Galvanometer: An instrument that can detect a weak electric current.

Faraday attached the ends of a coil of wire to a **galvanometer** (gal-vah-**nom**-et-ter). A *galvanometer* is an instrument that can detect a weak electric current. If an electric current is present, the needle on the galvanometer moves. Faraday moved a magnet back and forth inside the coil of wire. When he did this, the needle on the galvanometer moved, showing that an electric current was present in the wire.

Faraday concluded that moving a magnet inside a coil of wire will produce current electricity in the coil. Here is an activity in which you will do an experiment similar to Faraday's. However, your galvanometer will be a compass. A compass needle moves if an electric current is present.

ACTIVITY

A. Wrap one piece of wire around the cardboard roll as shown in picture 1. Wrap the other piece of wire around the compass as shown in picture 2. Make sure you can still see the compass needle. Leave about 30 cm (12 in.) of wire at each end.

B. Attach the ends of the wires as shown in picture 3.

C. Remove the tissue roll by sliding it outward.

D. Move the bar magnet back and forth inside the coil of wire. As you move the magnet, look at the compass needle.

1. What happened to the compass needle? Why?

E. Hold the magnet still inside the coil of wire. Look at the compass needle.

2. What happened to the compass needle? Why?

Materials
bar magnet
compass
cardboard roll
2 pieces of wire, 90 cm (36 in.) long

1

2

3

When you moved the magnet back and forth inside the wire coil, the compass needle moved. The compass needle moved because an electric current was present in the wire. The electric current was produced in the wire by the moving magnet. When the magnet was held still in the coil of wire the compass needle did not move. The compass needle did not move because no current was present in the wire.

How is the discovery that magnetism produces current electricity useful to us? Look at the drawing below. The drawing shows a machine called a **generator** (jen-err-ray-tore). In a *generator*, current electricity is produced with magnetism. A generator has four basic parts. It has a coil of wire called an **armature** (ar-mah-chur), one or more horseshoe magnets, two metal rings, and metal brushes. The *armature* is located between the poles of the horseshoe magnets. Turning the crank causes the armature to move between the poles of the magnet. In large generators, the magnet moves in and out of, or through, the armature. The metal rings connected to the end of the coil collect the current produced in the armature. The brushes lead the current out of the generator.

Generator: A machine in which current electricity is produced with magnetism.

Armature: The coil of wire in a generator.

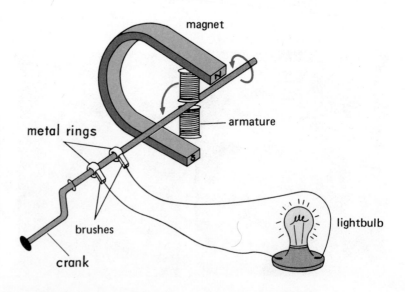

magnet

armature

metal rings

brushes

crank

lightbulb

The generator shown in the drawing on page 282 is a hand generator. It produces enough current electricity to light one lightbulb. Large generators located at power plants produce the current electricity needed to light the thousands of lightbulbs in your town or city.

MAIN IDEAS

Magnetism can produce current electricity. A generator is a machine in which current electricity is produced by a magnet moving through an armature or an armature moving between the poles of a magnet.

QUESTIONS

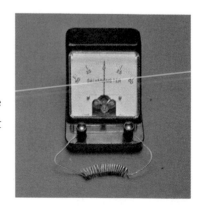

Write your answers on a sheet of paper.

1. How can you produce current electricity in the wire shown here? How will you know if an electric current is present in the wire?
2. What are the four basic parts of a generator?
3. Explain how a generator produces current electricity.

CHAPTER
USING ELECTRICITY

1 PRODUCING ELECTRICITY

Mark's teacher just asked the class how the coil or magnet in a generator can be made to turn. What idea does Mark have? What do you think about his idea?

When you finish this lesson, you should be able to:

○ List and describe three sources of energy used to turn parts of generators.

○ Tell the name given to a power plant at which falling water causes parts of generators to turn.

Mark's idea about a generator would not work very well. The mouse would get tired and stop because it does not have enough energy to keep the parts of the generator moving. A mouse is not a good source of energy. The energy needed to turn parts of large generators comes from many sources.

A long time ago people found that falling water was a source of energy. Falling water was used to turn large water wheels. The first water wheels made were used at grain mills to grind wheat into flour. Today falling water is used to turn water wheels called **turbines** (**tur**-binz). *Turbines* are used at power plants to turn parts of large generators.

Turbines: Water wheels used at power stations.

Most power plants are located near waterfalls or dams. Some of the water goes over the waterfall or dam and flows down the river. Some of the water is directed into large pipes. The water moves down through the pipes to turbines in the power plant. The falling water causes the turbines to spin. A rod connected to the turbines turns. The other end of the rod is connected to the magnets or coils of wire in the generator. The turning rod causes the coil or magnet to turn. As a result current electricity is produced in the generator.

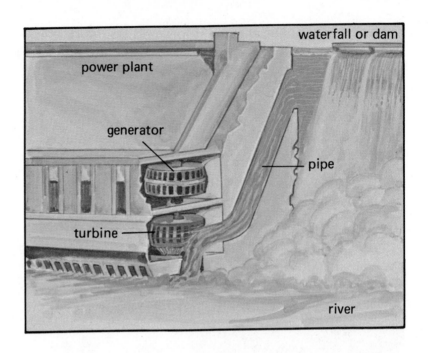

A power plant at which falling water is the energy source for producing electricity is called a **hydroelectric** (hi-dro-ee-**lek**-trik) plant. The word *hydro* means *water*. The picture below shows a *hydroelectric* plant at Niagara Falls, Canada.

Hydroelectric plant: A power plant at which falling water is the energy source.

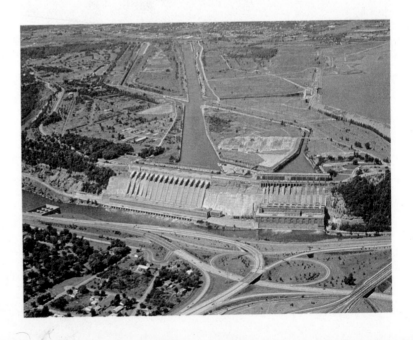

Energy to turn parts of generators also comes from the burning of fuel (**few**-ell). A *fuel* is anything that can be burned to produce heat. Oil, gas, and coal are examples of fuels. The heat from the burning fuel is used to change water into steam. The steam provides the energy needed to turn parts of the generator. Look at the drawing below. The water heated in the boiler changes to steam. The steam causes blades on the steam turbine to spin. The spinning blades turn a rod connected to the generator. As a result, current electricity is produced.

Scientists have found that a great amount of heat is produced in a **nuclear reaction** (**new**-klee-are ree-ak-shun). A *nuclear reaction* occurs when tiny particles of matter are split apart. The heat from the reaction can be used to change water into steam. At a nuclear power plant the heat from a nuclear reaction is the energy source for producing electricity.

Fuel: Anything that can be burned to produce heat.

Nuclear reaction: A reaction that occurs when tiny particles of matter are split.

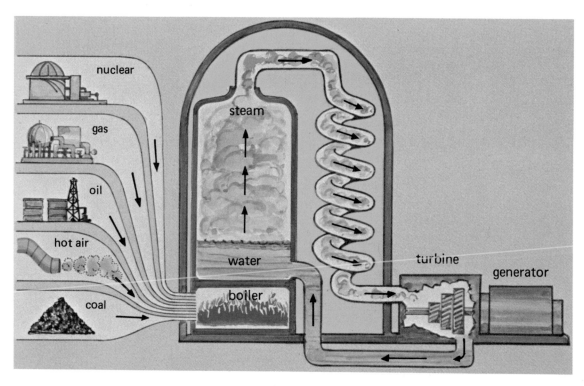

Turbines are used at power plants to turn parts of large electromagnets. Falling water, fuels, and a nuclear reaction can supply the energy needed to turn turbines.

QUESTIONS

Write your answers on a sheet of paper.

1. Energy to turn parts of generators comes from three sources. List the three sources.
2. Describe how falling water turns parts of generators that produce current electricity.
3. How do fuels and nuclear reactions turn parts of generators?
4. What name is given to a power plant at which falling water causes parts of generators to turn?

SOMETHING EXTRA

The use of nuclear reactions as an energy source for producing electricity began in 1957. In that year the first nuclear power plant went into operation. It was located at Shippingport, Pennsylvania. It now supplies electricity to the Pittsburgh area. Canada's first nuclear power plant began to produce electricity in 1962 at Rolphton, Ontario. Today, there are over 100 nuclear power plants in operation. Most are built near rivers or lakes because large amounts of water are needed to cool the generator.

Most of the nuclear power plants in the United States are owned by private utility companies. However, their operation is regulated by the Nuclear Regulatory Commission, a government agency.

2 CHANGING ELECTRICAL ENERGY

The man in the picture above is frying eggs in an electric frying pan. The frying pan uses electricity, but what causes the eggs to fry?

When you finish this lesson, you should be able to:

○ List four forms of energy that electricity can change to.

○ Identify the forms of energy involved in examples of energy changes.

The eggs fry when heated. However, the pan is not over a flame on a stove. Where did the heat come from?

Electricity is a form of energy. Sometimes electrical energy changes to other forms of energy. Electrical energy changes to heat energy that fries the eggs.

The first picture below shows an example of electrical energy changing to heat energy. Sometimes electricity produces so much heat that light is given off too. This occurs in a toaster. Electricity flowing through the wires in a toaster causes the wires to get hot. The wires get so hot that they glow, or give off light. Therefore, electrical energy can also change to light energy.

Electricity can be used to produce motion. The energy of motion is called **mechanical energy** (meh-kan-eh-kul). Electrical energy is changed to *mechanical energy* by motors. For example, the motor in an electric fan causes the blades of the fan to move. The motor changes electrical energy to mechanical energy (the motion of the blades).

Mechanical energy: The energy of motion.

Is there a doorbell at the front door of your house? What happens when someone presses the button of the doorbell? How do you think the sound is made? Look at the diagram below. The doorbell is part of a circuit. The circuit also has an electromagnet and a source of electric current. When the doorbell button is pressed, it touches one end of the metal clapper, closing the circuit. The clapper is pulled toward the electromagnet. The clapper strikes the bell as it moves toward the electromagnet and a sound is made. A ringing doorbell is an example of electrical energy changing to sound energy.

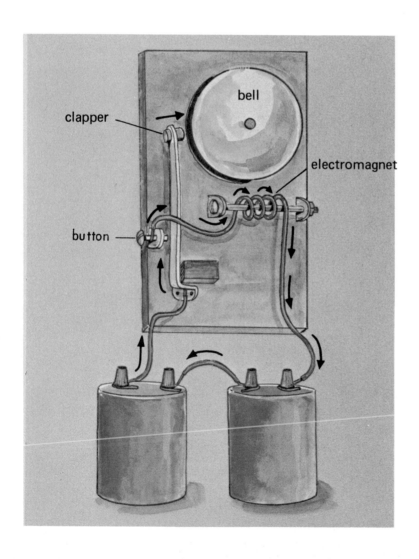

Sometimes electrical energy can change to several forms of energy at the same time. For example, a television operates on electrical energy. When your television is on, what do you see? What do you hear? If you touch the back of the television, what do you feel? Electrical energy changes to light, sound, and heat energy.

MAIN IDEAS

Electrical energy can change to other forms of energy. Electricity flowing through wires produces heat and light energy. Motors change electrical energy to mechanical energy. Electrical energy can also change into sound energy.

QUESTIONS

Write your answers on a sheet of paper.

1. List four forms of energy that electrical energy can change into.
2. Identify the forms of energy involved in the energy change that occurs in each example below:
   a. a doorbell
   b. an electric mixer
   c. a television
   d. a telephone
   e. a lightbulb

3 CONSERVING ELECTRICITY

Electricity is very useful. Many of the things you use for work and play are electrical. The girl shown above is playing an electric guitar. One of the boys is playing with electric trains. The woman is working with an electric calculator. Imagine the amount of electricity that would be used if every family was like the one shown above. How can the amount of electricity used in a household be measured? How and why should people control their use of electricity?

When you finish this lesson, you should be able to:

○ Describe how the amount of electricity used can be measured.

○ Explain why and how people should limit their use of electricity.

○ Tell how the production of electricity may be harmful to the environment.

Watt: The unit of measurement for how fast electrical energy is used.

Kilowatt-hour: The amount of kilowatts used in one hour.

The amount of electricity used in a household depends on how fast and how long the electricity is used. A **watt** is the unit of measurement for how fast electrical energy is used. If 1,000 *watts* are used, then a kilowatt has been used. The amount of kilowatts used in one hour is a **kilowatt-hour.** As electric current enters a house, it flows through an electric meter. The meter shows how many *kilowatt-hours* were used. Here is an activity in which you will read an electric meter.

Materials
paper
pencil

A. On your paper, draw two groups of four boxes next to one another as shown.

B. Look at the number on the front of the electric meter shown in the first picture. Write the number in the first group of boxes, one digit in each box.

C. Look at the number on the front of the electric meter shown in the second picture. Write the number in the second group of boxes.

D. Subtract the number in the first group of boxes from the number in the second group.
   1. What is the remainder?

The number shown on each meter indicates the kilo-watt-hours used. The pictures are of the same meter and were taken one month apart. How many kilowatt-hours were used in one month? If the cost for each kilowatt-hour is six cents, how much money will be paid for the usage? The picture below shows a monthly bill for the use of electricity. The bill shows the kilowatt-hours used during a certain length of time and the cost of the usage.

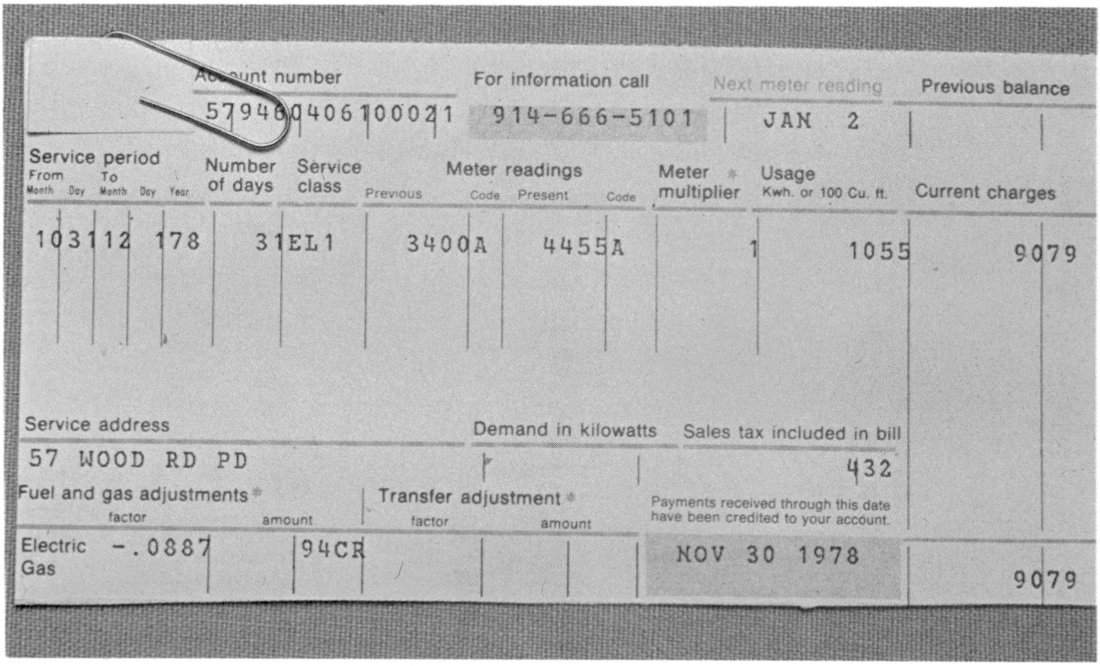

Account number	For information call	Next meter reading	Previous balance
57946 0406 100021	914-666-5101	JAN 2	

Service period From To Month Day Month Day Year	Number of days	Service class	Meter readings Previous	Code	Present	Code	Meter multiplier	Usage Kwh. or 100 Cu. ft.	Current charges
10 31 12 1 78	31	EL1	3400A		4455A		1	1055	9079

Service address		Demand in kilowatts	Sales tax included in bill
57 WOOD RD PD			432

Fuel and gas adjustments * factor amount	Transfer adjustment * factor amount	Payments received through this date have been credited to your account.	
Electric −.0887 94CR		NOV 30 1978	
Gas			9079

The electricity that enters your house is produced by a generator at a power plant. Oil, gas, and coal are often the energy sources used to operate the generator. Oil, gas, and coal are **natural resources**. A *natural resource* is something found in nature that is useful. However, the supplies of these natural resources are limited. Until new supplies are found or other energy sources developed, people must try to make the present supplies last. Limiting the use of electricity will conserve the supplies of natural resources.

Natural resource: Something found in nature that is useful.

295

One way to conserve energy is to use less electricity. Do you turn off the lights when you are the last person to leave a room? Does a television or radio remain on when no one in the house is watching or listening? If everyone used just a little less electricity, a great amount of energy would be saved. Using less electricity conserves the supplies of natural resources.

The burning of fuels to produce electricity can be harmful to the environment. The burning of oil, gas, and coal can cause **pollution** (pol-**loo**-shun). *Pollution* is the adding of harmful materials to the environment. For example, burning coal or oil releases substances such as **sulfur oxides** (sul-fur **ahk**-sides) into the air. *Sulfur oxides* can cause respiratory diseases in humans.

Pollution: The adding of harmful materials to the environment.

Sulfur oxides: Substances released when coal or oil are burned.

If oil is burned to produce electricity it is necessary to ship the oil to the place where it is burned. Sometimes, oil tankers that carry the oil spill their cargo. Oil spills pollute the water and harm the animal and plant life in and near the water.

One way to stop the pollution of the environment is to limit the use of the fuels by conserving electricity. Another way to stop pollution is to produce electricity by methods other than the burning of fuel. The use of falling water and nuclear energy are two other methods.

Nuclear energy does not pollute the air with sulfur oxides and smoke. However, it can affect the environment in other ways. For example, nuclear materials and wastes from the production of electricity are stored at power plants. Many people are concerned that these materials and wastes may enter the air or water if some problem occurs at the power plant. These materials and wastes can harm and even kill plant and animal life.

MAIN IDEAS

The amount of electricity people use depends on how fast and how long they use the electricity. Limiting the use of electricity will conserve the supplies of natural resources. The burning of fuels to produce electricity can cause pollution.

QUESTIONS

Write your answers on a sheet of paper.

1. What is a kilowatt? a kilowatt-hour?
2. What device measures the amount of electricity used in a household?
3. Why will limiting the use of electricity conserve the supplies of natural resources?
4. What is one way in which you could conserve electrical energy?
5. Tell how the production of electricity can pollute our environment.
6. Tell why nuclear energy may be a better method than burning fuels to produce electricity. Also tell a reason why it may not be a better method.

All matter contains tiny electrical particles. The electrical property of each particle is called a charge. Some electrical particles have a negative charge, and others have a positive charge. Like charges repel each other. Unlike charges attract each other. Static electricity is produced in an object that gains or loses negative charges.

When negative electric charges move from one place to another, current electricity is produced. The path through which negative charges flow is called a circuit. A circuit has a source of electric charges, materials through which the charges flow, and a user of the electricity.

In a series circuit there is only one path through which electric charges can flow. In a parallel circuit there is more than one path through which the charges can flow.

The space around a magnet is called a magnetic field. There is also a magnetic field around a wire through which current is flowing.

Current electricity can produce magnetism. Magnetism can produce current electricity. Falling water, fuels, and nuclear reactions supply the energy needed to operate generators that produce electricity. Limiting the use of electricity will conserve the supplies of these resources.

CHECK YOURSELF

Write your answers on a sheet of paper.
  1. What type of electricity is produced in an object that gains or loses negative charges?
  2. What happens when two negatively charged objects are brought close together?

3. What is current electricity? What is a circuit?
4. Give two examples of a conductor and an insulator.
5. Why doesn't a lightbulb in an open circuit light?
6. Name and describe two types of circuits.
7. Draw a circuit diagram of a parallel circuit that has two dry cells, two lightbulbs, and a closed switch.
8. What are lines of force?
9. What is a magnetic field?
10. How can you make an electromagnet? List three ways in which you can increase the strength of an electromagnet.
11. How is current electricity produced in a generator?
12. What energy source is used to produce electricity at a hydroelectric plant?
13. List three fuels that can be burned to produced electricity.
14. Give an example of a device in which electrical energy is changed to another form of energy.
15. What is a kilowatt-hour?
16. How does the burning of coal or oil pollute the environment? How might the use of nuclear energy to produce electricity be harmful?
17. List three ways you could conserve electricity.

PROJECTS

1. The sun is an energy source for producing electricity. Find out about solar energy. How can solar energy be changed to electrical energy? How can the use of solar energy conserve other natural resources?
2. Benjamin Franklin was a great statesman and scientist. Find out about Franklin's famous kite and key experiment. Library and research books will be helpful. When did Franklin do his experiment? How did he do the experiment? What did he discover?

4 crayons = 38.6 grams

THINK METRIC

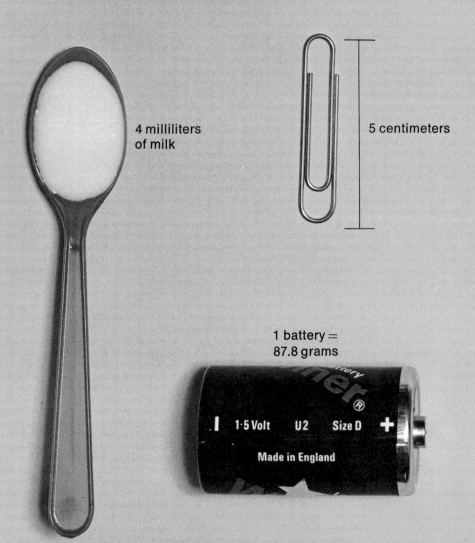

4 milliliters
of milk

5 centimeters

1 battery =
87.8 grams

1·5 Volt   U2   Size D   +

Made in England

3 jacks = 5.5 grams

4 of these = about 1 liter

13.75 centimeters

GLOSSARY/INDEX

production of, 284–288; *See also* Electricity.

Cygnus (**sig**-nes): a constellation, 234, 236

Decibels (**dess**-si-bells): units of measurement of sound intensity, 78

Deneb (**den**-ebb): a white star, 234

Desalination (dee-sal-lin-**nay**-shun): the process of removing salt from ocean water, 36

Dietician (die-et-**tish**-shun): a person who plans meals that contain all the nutrients, 157

Digestive system (die-**jes**-tiv): the system that changes food into a liquid the body can use, 164, 198

Drugs, use of, 145–147, 196, 197

Ear, parts of, 111–113

Ear canal: a narrow tube inside your ear that carries sound vibrations into your head, 111

Eardrum: the part of your ear at the end of the ear canal, 112

Earth, distance of stars from, measurement of, 229; distance from sun (chart), 222; importance of sun to, 225; life on, 217, 225; as planet, 203, 215; revolution of, 203–207, 250; revolution of moon around, 208, 212; rotation of, 203, 250; shape of, 203

Echo (**ek**-ko): a sound reflected from an object, 91–93, 98

Echo sounder: an instrument that sends out sounds that hit the ocean bottom, 48, 49

Eclipse (ee-**klips**), lunar, 212, 213, 250; solar, 212, 213, 226, 250

Edison, Thomas A., phonograph invented by, 95–96

Electric charges, 255–257, 298

Electric circuits, 258–259, 261; closed, 259; diagrams of, 265; open, 259; parallel, 266–268, 298; series, 262–265, 298

Electric meter, reading of, 294–295

Electrical energy, changing to other forms of energy, 289–292; conservation of, 293–297

Electricians (ee-lek-**trish**-unz), work done by, 261

Electricity, conservation of, 293–297; current (*See* Current electricity.); discovery of, 252; as form of energy, 289–292; static, 254–257, 298

Electromagnets: magnets made with current electricity, 277–279, 288, 291

Energy (**en**-err-jee): the ability to do work, 153/electricity as form of, 289–292; falling water as source of, 285, 288, 298; food and, 153, 155, 159; glucose and oxygen as producers of, 176, 177; heat, 289–290, 292; light, 290, 292; mechanical, 290, 292; nuclear, 287, 288, 296–298; solar, 226, 227; sound, 291, 292

Esophagus (eh-**sof**-ah-guss): the tube between your mouth and stomach, 162, 164

Excretory system (ex-**kreh**-tore-ree): the system that removes wastes from the body, 186, 198

Exercise, importance of, 144, 147, 148

Extinct (ex-**stinkt**): does not exist anymore, 44

Eye, parts of, 107–109

Faraday, Michael, 280–281

Fish, 38–40, 45

Food, 152–160; balanced diet, 157, 159, 160; bread-cereal group, 157; calories supplied by, 159, 160; carrying to cells, 166–169; digestion of, 161–165; and energy, 153, 155, 159; importance of, 143, 147, 148, 152–155; meat group, 157; milk group, 157; nutrients in, 153–155, 198; from ocean, 32–33; school lunch, 156, 157; testing for starch, 154, 155; vegetable-fruit group, 157

Food chain: a pattern of who-eats-whom, 39

Muscular system: all the muscles in your body, 138, 141, 148

Musical instruments, sounds produced by, 63–67, 84–88, 98

NASA (National Aeronautics and Space Administration), 223

Natural gas: a fossil fuel, 34

Natural resources: things found in nature that are useful, 295/conservation of, 295, 297

Neap tides (neep): low tides that are not very low; high tides that are not very high, 30

Nebula (neb-you-lah): clouds of dust and gas, 239, 240

Nephrons (nef-frons): tiny filters in the kidneys, 185

Neptune (nep-tune): an outer planet, 219, 221, 222

Nerve cells: cells that carry information from your sense organs to your brain, 103–105, 108, 119

Nerves, auditory, 112, 113; olfactory, 104, 105; optic, 108, 109; taste, 116

Nervous system: your sense organs, nerves, brain, and spinal cord, 122, 148

Nicotine (nik-koe-teen): a poisonous substance in tobacco, 146, 188

North Star (*See* Polaris.)

Northern Lights, 213

Nose, and respiration, 180–182; and sense of smell, 102-104

Nostrils (noss-trillz): the openings in your nose, 104

Nuclear energy, 287, 288, 296–298

Nuclear power plants, 287, 297

Nuclear reaction (new-klee-are ree-ak-shun): a reaction that occurs when tiny particles of matter are split, 287, 288

Nucleus (new-klee-us): part of a cell, 139

Nutrients (new-tree-ents): chemicals that your body needs for growth, repair, and energy, 153–155, 198

Ocean bottom, parts of, 2–6, 50; sediments on, 10, 11, 48, 49

Ocean floor: the part of the ocean bottom that begins where the continental slope ends, 4, 5, 50/changes in, 12–16; spreading of, 12–14, 16

Oceanographers (oh-shun-nog-graf-furs): scientists who study the oceans, 6, 48, 49

Oceans, currents in (*See* Currents.); desalination of water, 36; evaporation of water, 8, 9; exploration of, 46–50; farming in, 33, 36; food chain in, 39; fossil fuels from, 34, 36; heated by sun, 8, 20, 21; living things in, 37–40, 50; pollution of water, 41–45, 50; resources in, 32–36, 50; saltiness of water, reason for, 8–9, 20; tides in, 27–31; waves in, 22–26

Oersted, Hans Christian, 274, 275

Oil spills, 42, 43, 45

Olfactory nerve (ohl-fack-tore-ree): the nerve that carries smell messages to your brain, 104, 105

Open circuit, 259

Optic nerve (op-tick): the nerve that carries sight messages to your brain, 108, 109

Orbit (or-bit): the path of an object in space around another, 215

Orion (oh-rye-on): a constellation, 234, 236

Orion nebula, 239

Our Galaxy (Milky Way), 238–240, 250

Outer ear: the part of your ear that gathers sound vibrations, 111

Oxygen (ox-si-jen): a gas in the air the body uses, 175–177, 179, 181, 182, 198

Parallel circuit: a circuit with more than one path through which the charges can flow, 266–268, 298

Pelvis (pell-vis): the hip bones and backbone, 127

Percussion instruments: instruments made of solid material or material stretched over a container, 66, 98

Pesticides (pes-tih-sides): chemicals sprayed on crops, 42

Petroleum (peh-troll-lee-um): a fossil fuel, 34

Phases (fay-zez): the shapes the moon appears to be, 211, 213

Phonograph, first, 95–96

Physical therapists (fizz-eh-kal ther-ah-pists), 128

Pitch: the highness or lowness of a sound, 82, 83, 98/changing of, 84–88

Pivot joint: a kind of joint, 131

Planets: solid bodies in space that do not give off their own light, 203/distance of from sun (chart), 222; inner, 214–218, 250; orbits of, 215, 218; outer, 219–223, 250; revolution time (chart), 222; rotation time (chart), 222; *See also names of planets.*

Plankton: tiny plants and animals on the ocean surface, 38–40

Pluto (plu-toe): an outer planet, 219, 221, 222

Polaris (pole-ar-ess): a star always above Earth's North Pole, 235, 236/distance from Earth (chart), 229

Pollution (poe-loo-shun): the adding of harmful materials to something, 41/of air, 296, 297; of ocean water, 41–45, 50

Protein (pro-teen): a nutrient needed for growth and repair of the body, 155/food sources for (chart), 153

Proxima Centauri (prox-eh-ma sen-tor-ee), distance from Earth (chart), 229

Pulse (puls): the spurting of blood past a place in an artery, 172, 173

Pupil (pew-pull): the opening in the center of your iris, 107, 109

Radio telescope, 244, 245, 250

Rarefaction (rare-eh-fak-shun): the spreading out of air particles, 61, 98

Receiver: the part of the telephone through which you hear, 95

Receptors (ree-sep-tores): nerve cells in your skin, 119, 121, 122

Reed: the piece of wood in the mouthpiece of a woodwind, 64

Reflect: to bounce off an object, 90

Reflected sounds, 90–93, 98

Reflecting telescope (ree-flek-ting): a telescope in which light is reflected, 243, 245, 250

Refracting telescope (ree-frak-ting): a telescope in which light is bent, 242, 245, 250

Repel (ree-pell): to move away from, 256

Respiratory system (res-pu-rah-tore-ee): the system that takes in and gives off gases, 182, 198

Rest, importance of, 144, 147, 148

Retroreflector (ret-tro-ree-flek-tore): a piece of equipment used by astronauts, 248, 249

Revolve (ree-volv): to move around something, 203

Ribs: twelve pairs of bones, 127

Rigel (rye-jel): a blue star, 234/color and temperature of (chart), 230

Rotate (row-tate): to spin, 203

Saliva (sa-lie-vah): a liquid in your mouth that moistens food, 162

Satellite (sat-tell-lite): an object in space that revolves around a planet, 208

Saturn (sat-turn): an outer planet, 219, 220, 222

Sea anemone (ah-nem-oh-nee): an ocean animal, 38, 40

Sea of Serenity (sir-**ren**-it-tee): a smooth area on the moon's surface, 209

Sea of Tranquility (tran-**kwil**-it-tee): a smooth area on the moon's surface, 209

Seasons, reasons for changes in, 204–207, 250

Sediments (**sed**-eh-ments): sand, clay, and other materials that settle in water, 10, 11, 48, 49

Sense organs: parts of your body that pick up information about the things you smell, see, hear, taste, and touch, 103

Senses, 102–122; hearing, 110–113; sight, 106–109; smell, 102–105; taste, 114–117; touch, 118–122

Series circuit: a circuit with only one path through which the charges can flow, 262–265, 298

Sewage (**sue**-ij): waste materials carried by sewers and drains, 42

Sewage treatment plants, 42

Sight, sense of, 106–109

Sirius (**sir**-ee-us), color and temperature of (chart), 230; distance from Earth (chart), 229

Skeletal muscle: a type of muscle, 140, 141

Skeletal system (**skel**-eh-tal): all the bones in your body, 125, 128, 148

Skin, 119, 121, 122

Small intestine (in-**tes**-tin): a long tube that food enters when the food leaves the stomach, 164

Smell, sense of, 102–105

Smoking, harmful effects of, 146–148, 187–191

Smooth muscle: a type of muscle, 139, 141

Sodium chloride (**so**-dee-um **klor**-ide): a salt, 8

Solar eclipse (**so**-lar ee-**klips**): occurs when the moon passes between Earth and the sun, 212, 213, 226, 250

Solar energy, 226, 227

Solar flares: bright areas in the sun's atmosphere from which hot gases shoot out, 225, 227

Solar system: the nine planets, their moons, and the sun, 215, 250/*See also* Planets; Sun.

Solids, travel of sound through, 69–71, 74, 75, 98

Sonic boom, 75

Sound(s), absorption of, 92; echoes, 91–93, 98; frequency of, 81, 82; intensity of, 76–79, 98; media for, 69–71, 74, 75, 98; musical instruments as producers of, 63–67, 84–88, 98; phonograph recording of, 95–96; pitch of, 82–88, 98; reflected, 90–93, 98; sonic boom, 75; speed of, 72–75, 98; telephone and, 94–95, 97; ultrasonic, 82, 83, 91–93; vibrations and, 56, 57, 60, 62–67, 82, 86–88, 98, 111, 113

Sound energy, 291, 292

Sound-level meter, 78

Sound movie, first, 62

Sound track, 62

Sound wave: a series of compressions and rarefactions, 61–62, 98

Space travel, 246–249; *Eagle,* 246, 248; *Explorer I,* 246; *Friendship 7,* 247; by Soviet Union, 246, 247, 249; *Sputniks,* 246; *Viking I,* 214, 218

Spallanzani, Lazzaro, experiment with bats, 89, 91

Spinal cord (**spy**-nal **cord**): a large nerve that carries messages to your brain, 121, 122

Spring tides: very high and very low tides, 30

Starch, food sources for (chart), 153; testing food for, 154, 155

Stars: objects in space made of hot gases, 224, 228–240/brightness of, 230; color of, differences in, 230;

constellations, 232–236, 250; distance from Earth, measurement of, 229; dwarfs, 229; galaxies, 237–240, 250; giants, 229; magnitude of, 230; super giants, 229; *See also names of stars.*

Static electricity: a type of electricity produced when objects gain or lose charges, 254–257, 298

Stethoscope (**steth**-oh-scope): an instrument used to hear heartbeats, 70

Stomach, 162–164

Stringed instruments: instruments with one or more strings, 63, 86, 98

Submarine canyon (sub-mar-een **kan**-yon): a groove cut in the continental shelf and slope, 10, 11

Sulfur oxides (sul-fur **ak**-sidz): substances released when coal or oil are burned, 296

Summer solstice (**sole**-stis): the first day of summer in the Northern Hemisphere, 204

Sun, 224–227; color and temperature of (chart), 230; corona of, 226, 227; currents caused by, 20, 21; distance of from planets (chart), 222; eclipse of, 212, 213, 226, 250; energy from, 226, 227; gases on, 225; life on Earth dependent on, 225; ocean water heated by, 8, 20, 21; planets closest to, 215–218; planets farthest from, 219–223; revolution of Earth around, 203–207; as star, 224, 250

Sunspots: dark spots on the sun, 225, 227

Supersonic transport (SST), 75

Tar: a poisonous substance in tobacco, 146, 188

Taste, sense of, 114–117

Taste buds: groups of cells on your tongue, 116, 117

Taste nerves: nerves that carry taste messages to your brain, 116

Telegraph, invention of, 279

Telephone, 94–95, 97

Telescopes (**tell**-eh-scopes): instruments used to study distant objects, 242–245, 250

Tendons (**ten**-dahns): attach muscles to bones, 135, 141

Tereshkova, Valentina (val-en-tee-nah tear-ish-**koh**-vah), 247, 249

Thunder, 74

Tides: the rise and fall of ocean water, 28–31

Tobacco, harmful effects of, 146–148, 187–191

Tongue, 116, 117

Touch, sense of, 118–122

Trachea (**tray**-key-ah): the windpipe at the back of the throat, 180–182

Trade winds: winds that blow from east to west toward the equator, 19, 21

Transmitter: the part of the telephone you speak into, 95

Trenches: deep ocean valleys, 12, 14

Tricep (**try**-sep): the muscle on the bottom side of your upper arm, 134, 141

Trough (**troff**): the lowest point of a wave, 23, 24, 26

Tsunamis (soo-**nahm**-mees): giant waves, 26

Turbines (**tur**-binz): water wheels used at power stations, 285, 288

Tycho (**tie**-ko): a crater on the moon, 209

Ultrasonic (uhl-tra-**son**-ick): having a frequency greater than 20,000 vibrations per second, 82

Ultrasonic sounds, 82, 83, 91–93

Universe (**you**-nih-vers): all the galaxies and the space they occupy, 240/formation of, theories explaining, 240

PHOTO CREDITS

HRW Photos by William Hubbell appear on pages: 32, 54, 58, 59, 62–64, 67, 69, 70, 71, 76, 81, 82, 84, 86–88, 90, 93, *right* 96, 102, 113–115, 123, 127–129, 132, 133, 135, 143–145, 152, 154, 156, 159, 160, 162, 166, 170, 172, 176, 179, 183, 184, 191–193, 196, 202, 205, 210, 224, 230, 248, 255, 256, 258–261, 263, 264, 266, 267, 271, 272, 275, 276, 278, 280, 281, *bottom* 283, 289, 290, 295.

HRW Photos by Russel Dian appear on pages: 79, 107, 119, 120, 174, *right* 200, 201, 270.

Cover Copyright by the California Institute of Technology and Carnegie Institution of Washington. Reproduced by permission from the Hale Observatories.

Unit 1: p. 1—Alan Pitcairn from Grant Heilman; p. 7—Miguel/The Image Bank; p. 8—USDA Soil Conservation Service; p. 12—Rare Book Division/The New York Public Library/Astor, Lenox and Tilden Foundations; p. 15—Ted Ramos; p. 16—UPI; p. 17—Map Division/The New York Public Library/Astor, Lenox and Tilden Foundations; p. 22—John Zimmerman/EPG; p. 25—John Serafin/Peter Arnold, Inc.; p. 26—NOAA; p. 27—Russ Kinne/Photo Researchers; p. 34—Shell Oil Company; p. 38—*left* Bob Evans/Peter Arnold, Inc.; *right* Edward E. Vaughan/Woodfin Camp & Associates; p. 40—Fritz Goro; p. 41—Frank Aleksandrowicz/EPA-Documerica; p. 42—*left* Daniel Brody/Editorial Photocolor Archives, Inc.; *right* USDA; p. 43—UPI; p. 45—Hope Alexander/EPA-Documerica; p. 46—Richard Steedman/The Image Bank; p. 47—Dan McCoy/Rainbow; p. 48—Woods Hole Oceanographic Institution; p. 49—Dan McCoy/Rainbow.

Unit 2: pp. 52–53—Dr. Richard Orville; p. 56—*left* Bob Barrett/The Image Bank; *right* Sylvia Johnson/Woodfin Camp & Associates; p. 65—Lawrence Fried/The Image Bank; p. 68—The Granger Collection; p. 72—Gale Constable/Focus on Sports; p. 75—Air France; p. 78—Bruel & Kjaer Precision Instruments, Inc.; p. 89—S.C. Bisserot/Bruce Coleman, Inc.; p. 94—Shostal Associates, Inc.; p. 97—Courtesy of Norlin Music, Inc.

Unit 3: pp. 100–101—Ringling Bros. and Barnum & Bailey; p. 103—Ward's Natural Science Establishment; p. 110—John Senzer; p. 125—*left* Marvin E. Newman/Woodfin Camp & Associates; *right* American Telephone and Telegraph Company; p. 142—Marvin E. Newman/Woodfin Camp & Associates; p. 146—USDA; p. 147—U.S. Department of Justice, Drug Enforcement Administration.

Unit 4: pp. 150–151—Star Wars. Copyright © 1977 Twentieth Century Fox Film Corp. All rights reserved; p. 178—The Bettmann Archive, Inc.; p. 187—Leo Stashin/Time-Life Picture Agency; p. 189—G.T. Hewlett 1972, Narcotics Education Inc.

Unit 5: p. 200—*left* Kitt Peak National Observatory; p. 209—NASA; p. 211—*left* Yerkes Observatory; *middle* Lick Observatory/University of California; *right* Hale Observatories; p. 213—NCAR; pp. 214, 216, 217—*left* NASA; p. 217—*right* University of Arizona/Lunar and Planetary Laboratory; p. 219—The Bettmann Archive, Inc.; p. 220—*top* NASA; *bottom* University of Arizona/Lunar and Planetary Laboratory; pp. 223, 225—NASA; p. 226—Los Alamos Scientific Laboratory; p. 227—Robert Phillips/Exxon Enterprises, Inc.; p. 228—Copyright by the California Institute of Technology and Carnegie Institution of Washington. Reproduced by permission from the Hale Observatories; p. 231—NASA; p. 239—*left* Photography by Orien A. Ernest, copyright © 1978 by AstroMedia Corp.; *right* Copyright by the California Institute of Technology and Carnegie Institution of Washington. Reproduced by permission from the Hale Observatories; p. 241—Lick Observatory/University of California; p. 243—Copyright by the California Institute of Technology and Carnegie Institution of Washington. Reproduced by permission from the Hale Observatories; p. 244—NASA; p. 245—The Bettmann Archive, Inc.; pp. 246–247—NASA.

Unit 6: pp. 253–253—Bruce Coleman, Inc.; p. 262—Courtesy Edward J. Mammen, Jr.; p. 269—UPI; p. 274—The Bettmann Archive, Inc.; p. 277—Grant Heilman; p. 279—The Bettmann Archive, Inc.; p. 283—*top* U.S. Department of Energy; p. 285—Mabry Mill, Blue Ridge Parkway, Va./Virginia State Travel Service; p. 286—Ontario Hydro; p. 288—Atomic Industrial Forum; p. 294—Duncan Electric Company, Inc.; p. 296—Leroy Woodson/EPA-Documerica.

ART CREDITS

Ed Algor, pages 121, 136, 168

Mel Erikson, pages 2, 3, 5, 9, 10, 11, 13, 14, 15, 21, 24, 33, 34, 37, 39, 48, 66, 74, 83, 91, 92, 108, 109, 111, 112, 124, 126, 130, 131, 134, 139, 140, 163, 165, 167, 168, 169, 171, 177, 178, 180, 181, 185, 195, 197, 203, 204, 232, 234, 238, 257, 286, 287, 291

Daniel Kirk, page 215

Vantage Art, Inc., pages 3, 18, 19, 20, 23, 25, 28, 29, 30, 31, 35, 39, 44, 55, 60, 61, 74, 78, 85, 95, 153, 157, 158, 175, 181, 188, 190, 194, 206, 212, 222, 229, 230, 233, 235, 236, 242, 243, 244, 260, 265, 268, 282

Jerry Zimmerman, pages 80, 118, 138, 161, 208, 237, 254, 281, 293